The ABC's of Typography

by SANDRA B. ERNST

Art Direction Book Company

Copyright © 1977, Sandra B. Ernst
Designed by Sandra B. Ernst
Revised 1984

Library of Congress Catalog Card Number:
77–80333
ISBN: 88108-010-1 (cloth)
ISBN: 88108-011-X (paper)

Published by
ART DIRECTION BOOK COMPANY
10 East 39th Street
New York, N.Y. 10016

Printed in the United States of America
Second Printing, 1986
Third Printing, 1990
Fourth Printing, 1992
Fifth Printing, 1994

Dedication

*This book is dedicated
to everyone who has found
that the type
doesn't fit.*

Acknowledgments

Special thanks to Vic Eisenhut and Graphic Arts, Inc. of Topeka for setting the majority of the type specimens. I'm particularly indebted to Gene Ernst for the artwork and sketches. Rosalind Gorton did a magnificent job of typing from the roughest of rough drafts.

John A. Krider, art director for the Office of University Publications, provided criticism and inspiration. Dr. Robert Bontrager, who was acting head of the department of journalism and mass communications at Kansas State University when I developed the first draft, provided administrative support while I tested several sections in a programmed instruction format. My thanks to him and to my students in those sections of the magazine production course.

Paul Freeman introduced me to the Society of Scribes and the work of contemporary calligraphers in New York. Ed Benguiat, type designer for ITC, conferred about computer typesetting and type design. Don Barron opened many doors and provided illustrations from The Art Direction Creativity series. Bill Parker, a master editor, waded through the maze of the manuscript and managed to keep the pieces straight.

Most of the type samples were set on Compugraphic Equipment, using licensed ITC faces. Other type suppliers, equipment manufacturers, and foundries represented in this book include: Zipatone, Prestype, Visual Graphics Corp., Letraset, Mecanorma, Type Films of Chicago, Ludlow, Artype, Bauer, Stempel, Haas, Nebiolo, Neufville, American Type Founders, Deberny Peignot, Monotype, Stephenson Blake, and Berthold.

Contents

Typography: An Art and a Science

Type is a creation of both art and science. Graphic designers look at type as a basic tool of their art. Writers look at type as a functional element of their message. Those who are untrained in either editing or design, look at type and probably don't even notice it. And that's the way it should be when the type works well with both the message and the design.

Typography is the one area that transcends all aspects of graphics—art, printing, and editing. The design of the words is as dear to the writer as to the artist; but because typography is so universal, it is also neglected. Excepting some prestige schools, there are few classes in typography. Such classes were once a requirement for journalism students, now they are seldom even available to them. Art students may take courses in graphic design, commercial illustration, even lettering—and still lack basic knowledge of the printed word and how it gets printed.

Since typography classes are rare, this book has been developed in a self-study format. It is for the student, as well as the working professional, for whom a typography class is not available. Since it is basic, it begins with rudimentary concepts. Designers may find the discussion of letter shapes simplistic; journalists may find the type measurements elementary; but as you get to the more advanced chapters, particularly in areas beyond your traditonal study, you will probably find interesting and challenging information for all levels and backgrounds.

One aspect of this book is unique: you will have the opportunity to develop some of the illustrations yourself. Type samples and other examples have been included to help you "see" the distinctions and differences, but space has been left for illustrations that you develop as a learning exercise. You will need a flat or chisel-point felt-tip marker, a chisel-point pencil or a broad italic pen for many of the exercises.

A number of questions have been included, also, so you can test yourself. These are set in italics. Space is provided for your calculations and answers. Answers to the questions of fact regarding type faces are given in the Appendix.

This is a pragmatic approach to basic typography. Discussions of equipment are kept to a minimum since today's machines may likely be obsolete before this book sees print. It's a how-to-do-it book—how to see differences in typefaces, how to specify, how to mark up and how to copyfit. The book's goal is to show you how to use type, not how to set it.

The ABC's of Typography

Chapter 1

Your Printer's Primer

The perception and processing of information through written symbols is a complex science and seldom recognized as art. Type can help communication but it can also impede understanding. For these reasons we encourage you to study typography—to appreciate the art and to understand the science.

Have you ever noticed all the different shapes we use for the letter G?

How did you ever learn to recognize such a variety of forms as one and the same letter? In contrast, a slight change in strokes can convert a *c* into an *e* or an *o*. Designing letterforms is as difficult a challenge as perceiving them.

The Basic Letter Distinctions

Letters differ in many ways. Size, shape, and slant are just a few of the distinctive features which give us thousands of variations. We will begin with some basics. Have patience if these remind you of Big Chief tablets and thumb-size pencils.

Capitals and Lower-Case—The most basic distinction is between upper- and lower-case letters—"big" and "small." The terms upper-case and lower-case come from early practices with hand-set type, the individual letters having been kept in wooden boxes known as type cases. Originally the capital letter cases were located above those for the small letters and since the Renaissance we have spoken of upper- and lower-case letters, even though most cases today have spaces for both kinds of letters.

UPPER lower

Slant. Another basic distinction is between upright letters and letters that slant to the right. We have come to call the slanting letters *italics* because slanted letters were used quite early in Italian calligraphy. Originally italic was a letter style all its own. In recent times italic has become a variation available with most typefaces.

EFMN *EFMN*

Zones. In basic lettering we usually draw guidelines to help maintain the proportion of the parts of the letters. These lines divide the letters into zones. For capitals, three guidelines are drawn which divide the letter into two zones.

1. *Using a wide, flat-pointed marker (chisel point felt-tip pen or pencil, or italic pen) and using the guidelines, letter your full name in capitals. Notice the proportion of the letter forms.*

The ABC's of Typography

A B C D E F
G H I J K L
M N O P Q R
S T U V W X
Y Z

Lower-case letters are based on four zones created by drawing five guidelines.

phe

2. *Letter your name in lower-case letters using the guidelines.*

a b c d e f
g h i j k l m
n o p q r s t
u v w x y z

When the guidelines for the upper- and lower-case letters are combined, they help you see the relationship between the two forms. These relationships differ with different typeface designs and this variety in basic relationships contributes to the individual personality of typefaces.

3. *Letter the name of this book using the guidelines.*

Coastlines. The top and bottom edges of the letters are called the coastlines. Upper-case letters have a straight coastline and lower-case letters have a variable coastline. We will use this term more in Chapter 8 when we discuss legibility.

The ABC's of Typography

The Parts of the Letter

Letters have three main parts: the x-height, which is the body; the ascender, which is any element sticking above the x-height; and the descender, which is the tail dropping below the x-height. These elements are important when you try to measure type or discriminate between two different typefaces.

x-height **acemnorsuvwxz**

ascenders **bdfhiklt**

descenders **gpqy j**

4. *Letter your full name in lower-case letters and study the pattern of ascenders, descenders, and x-heights. Draw the coastlines.*

The proportions between these three elements vary with different kinds of type. Some typefaces have small x-heights and long ascenders and descenders. Some have big x-heights and short descenders and ascenders.

Americana Harlech

5. *Copy the two typeface alphabets and maintain, as well as you can, the proportions of the x-heights and the ascenders and descenders.*

a. abcdefghijklmnopqrstuvwxyz
b. abcdefghijklmnopqrstuvwxyz

Look at the two faces in the alphabet samples. Do you think they are the same size? Because of the different proportions, the typeface on the top looks smaller, to some people, than the one on the bottom. In fact, they are the same size.

abpd abpd
a. b.

6. *Which of the two alphabets do you think is easier to read? a ___ b ___*

If you were trying to squeeze a lot of type onto one page, which type-face would you use?   a _____   b _____

Why?

Another example of the tricks letter proportion can play appears when *abpd* is set in two typefaces.

abcd   abcd
a.   b.

7. *Do you think the two typefaces are the same size?*

If not, which typeface is bigger?

The size of the face on the left is 30 point and that of the face on the right is 36 point. Even though the face on the left is smaller, the two may appear to be the same size because the x-height of the letters is almost the same in both.

8. *Letter the word "hope" in both typeface proportions. (You will need to draw in the x-height guidelines.)*

Swashes. Some letters have highly ornamented details which can be used as decorative touches at the beginning and ending of words and lines. These letters and their decorative accents are called "swashes." The swash letters *A, M,* and *R* are shown in the Bookman typeface:

9. Circle the swash letters in the typographic design, "So Buy Now."

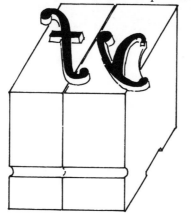

Kerns. Some letters have tails or other elements that create a problem when you're trying to set letters closely with a minimum of space between them. Printers solved this problem by "kerning" the letters. The kern pro-

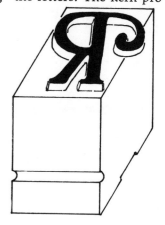

The ABC's of Typography

jects over the edge of the metal body. Early printers were reluctant to use kerns because they were delicate and could easily be broken off the metal body. With modern phototypesetting, this technical problem does not occur, and more kerns are being designed and specified by typographers. In modern typography we refer to kerned letters as any which project beyond the body at the sides. Such letters as *A, Y, T, V, W,* and *L* can be kerned. Most swash letters are kerned. The lower-case *f* was usually kerned as were the sloping strokes of the upper-case *W.*

WWAAMMW

Ligatures. Ligatures are single characters which contain two or more letters. They were common in early printing. A few have been carried through the years such as *fi, fl, ff.* Recently there has been a resurgence of ligatures and some contemporary faces have been designed with an assortment of ligatures.

CACEAFAFRGAHTKALALNTRRASSSTSTTHUT ff fi fl ffi ffl

Outlines. Letters need not be printed all-black. They can be outlined with a thin line and the inside of the space left blank. They can also be shadowed or shaded to give three-dimensional appearance. These two treatments also can be combined for a shadow outline.

Another variation on the outline technique is the "Inline." This style of letter has a white line reversed out of the black body.

Comstock

The Strokes of the Letter

Another way to describe a letter is by its strokes. The basic stroke of the letter is usually thick or wide or "strong"; other strokes may be thin and are called hairlines.

ONL

As you can see by studying these letters above there can be a difference in the width of the strokes. In some types of letters this is very pronounced; in others there is no difference at all. When you analyze a letter by its strokes, you will usually refer to the "thicks and thins" of the letter.

10. *Copy the letters ABC and pay particular attention to the contrast between thick and thin strokes.*

ABC

ABC

The two alphabets below illustrate the thick and thin strokes available in various type faces.

abcdefghijklmnopqrstuvwxyz
abcdefghijklmnopqrstuvwxyz

11. *Letter your name using a letter style that has very pronounced thick and thin strokes and another style that makes little distinction between thick and thin.*

Serifs

Serifs are the little cross-strokes at the ends of principal strokes. They are ornamental—a little flourish that signifies the termination of the stroke. Serifs are also functional. When the early Roman stonecutters hand-chiseled their beautifully proportioned letters, they found the end of the chisel line would be rough unless finished with a cross-stroke. A hori-

zontal serif at the foot of a letter also made a perfect baseline. The serif was bracketed into the principal line with a curving fillet. The medieval scribes used serifs for a different reason. The serif was made by the spread of the ink where the pen first touched the paper and by the blob of ink that remained after the basic stroke. Serifs may be concave and convex, angled or flat/perpendicular/square, sharp or round, prominent or small, or even absent (sans serifs).

EEEEEE

12. *Copy the capital and lower-case alphabets illustrated and study the places where the serifs appear.*

ABCDEFGHIJKLMNOPQ RSTUVWXYZ abcdefgh ijklmnopqrstuvwxyz

Loops

Another distinctive feature of a letter is the slant of the loops. Some letters sit upright, others have a slant as determined by the axis of the loop. The best way to identify this slant is to look at the loops in the open letters such as o, c, and e.

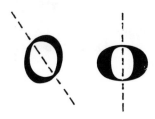

In some letters the set of the slant is obvious; in others you can hardly tell.

abcdefghijkl mnopqrstuvwxyz
abcdefghijklmnopqrstuvwxyz

13. *Letter your first name using two types of letters, one which has upright loops and one with slanted loops.*

Review

This discussion of basic letter forms may be elementary to some readers. Some may feel it too advanced. A quick review should bring everything together. We looked at six distinctive elements:

1. Case: upper or lower.
2. Slant: Upright or sloping.
3. The X-Height proportion: large on the body or small on the body.
4. Stroke: Uniform or pronounced thick and thin.
5. Serifs: Angled, flat, square, round, or absent (sans).
6. Loops: upright or slanted.

14. *Five kinds of type are shown in complete alphabets. Compare them with respect to six elements above.*

a. abcdefghijklmnopqrstuvwxyz

b. abcdefghijklmnopqrstuvwxyz

c. *abcdefghijklmnopqrstuvwxyz*

d. abcdefghijklmnopqrstuvwxyz

e. ABCDEFGHIJKLMNOPQRSTUVWXYZ

Typeface A:

1. _____
2. _____
3. _____
4. _____
5. _____
6. _____

The ABC's of Typography

Typeface B:

1. _____

2. _____

3. _____

4. _____

5. _____

6. _____

Typeface C:

1. _____

2. _____

3. _____

4. _____

5. _____

6. _____

Typeface D:

1. _____

2. _____

3. _____

4. _____

5. _____

6. _____

Typeface E:

1. _____

2. _____

3. _____

4. _____

5. _____

6. _____

Chapter 2

Composition

Putting type together is called composition or typesetting. It has always been a creative accomplishment, just as composition has been a creative aspect of writing and design. Early printers like William Caxton and Benjamin Franklin were compositors in both senses. In colonial times the printer molded the thought of his society as he held the "composing stick" in his hand and composed his message letter-by-letter. We still use the term composition for setting type—even though editors and designers have come between the printer and his words.

Calligraphy and Inscription

Our letters have been shaped by the tools used to write them. We have scratched them in sand with a stick, marked them in wax with a stylus, carved them in marble with a chisel, writen them on parchment with a quill, and printed them on paper with metal, cameras, and cathode-ray tubes. But the shape of the letter has changed very little since the early Romans first displayed their language in stone.

Inscription. With all our quills, pens, and machines we have been hard pressed to emulate the beauty of the letters Romans carved in stone more than 2,000 years ago. The Romans' letters were as finely proportioned as their columns. Like the columns, the Romans' letters were gently swelling shapes with delicate serifs to finish the letter lines. From a distance the letter form is uniform and highly readable—an example of perfectly proportioned form. The Romans' letters were also written using a brush, a reed, or a quill. Early scribes hand-lettered entire books.

ABCDEFGHIJKLMNOPQRSTU VWXYZ 1234567890

1. *Copy the Roman alphabet and pay particular attention to the serifs and the swelling of the strokes.*

Unicials. During the Middle Ages, the Roman letters were drawn in a highly rounded form which we call "unicials." These were popular from the Fourth to the Eighth century.

ABCDEFGHIJKLMNO PQRSTUVWXYZ

2. *With a broad-point pen or marker, copy the unicial alphabet.*

Italic. Until the time of Charlemagne the only alphabet was the capitals. Charlemagne's scribes encouraged the use of small letters, then called minuscules, in handwritten official records and documents. The Carolingian hand adapted the graceful handwriting of Italy and produced a type of writing eventually called italic. We use this term now to refer to a variation within a typeface, but it was originally a lettering style of its own.

$$abcdefghijklmnopqrstuvwxyz$$
$$ABCDEFGHHIJJKL$$
$$MNOPQRSTUVWXYZ$$

3. *With a broad-point pen or marker, copy the lower-case and capital italic alphabets.*

Black Letter. Commonly known as "black letter" because of its appearance, a type of letter which developed between the Eleventh and Thirteenth centuries is sometimes called "gothic" after the Goths from whom it was thought to be copied. It is also called "text" because of its use in manuscripts. This letter relies on broad angled strokes.

$$ABCDEFGHIJKLMNOPQRSTUV$$
$$WXYZ\ abcdefghijklmnopqrstuvwxyz$$

4. With a broad-point pen, copy the lower case black-letter alphabet.

_____

_____

_____

_____

_____

_____

Contemporary Calligraphy. Calligraphy did not die with the advent of movable type. Modern calligraphers are busy designing new typefaces and hand lettering posters and advertisements. Original calligraphy represents quality and it is a very expensive art form. Observe two examples of the hand drawn work of contemporary calligraphers and hand letterers.

Lubalin, Smith, Carnase

Arthur Baker

Hand-Set Type

In the Fifteenth century, Johann Gutenberg invented movable type and put an end to the hand-lettering of books and manuscripts. Within 25 years his invention had spread throughout Europe.

Metal and Wood Type. Metal type for hand setting differs little from that of Gutenberg's day. Each letter is individually cast in a lead alloy from a mold or matrix. The letters, which are cast in right-to-left reverse, are composed into words which read correctly after an inked impression has been made from their faces. A type foundry is the company which converts the type design into matrices and, from these, casts type for sale to typographers and printers. The type designed by Gutenberg was copied from the hand-drawn letters of his day—the "black letters." Gutenberg's and other early Bibles were printed in that type style.

Handset letters are still in use. Some printers still have their handset type from the turn of the century. One display typecasting machine uses handset matrix letters to form the mold from which a line is then cast for printing. The most frequent use of handset type is in small private presses operated by hobbyists. The time involved in handsetting words letter-by-letter is prohibitive for commercial printing. The real problem with handsetting is not so much the setting but the distributing of the type. Each piece of type has to be replaced into the type case. It's a dirty job that all printers hate.

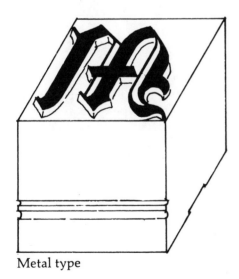

Metal type

Transfer type

Transfer Type. A modern version of handset type, transfer type is used primarily for display—headlines and titles. Transfer type is sold on acetate sheets that have a number of characters in both upper- and lower-case alphabets as well as numerals and punctuation marks.

There are two basic kinds of transfer letters. To use one kind, a pencil or burnisher is rubbed over the letter, which is on the back of the acetate sheet. The burnishing sticks the letter to the paper and releases it from the acetate. The second kind has the letter printed on a sheet of sticky acetate which is mounted on a heavier transparent backing. The printed letter is cut around with a knife and lifted off the backing. The letter can be positioned where wanted and even lifted up and moved around. The first kind doesn't allow that; once the letter is burnished in place, it's down for good. It can be removed with a piece of drafting tape, but you can't move it around.

Typographers look upon transfer sheets with some measure of scorn. But they are useful when your printer has a limited range of display faces. They are also cheap and easy to use on a small scale. You can design with them and develop typographic art even if you have no lettering skills yourself. You can also do things like close-setting of type, a technique which may not be available mechanically from your printer.

Squeeze Squeeze Squeeze

Hot-Metal Typesetting

It took more than 400 years before a machine was developed to set the movable type which Gutenberg invented. In the 1880's Ottmar Mergenthaler invented the Linotype, a machine which sets type at faster speeds than handset and automatically distributes the matrices from which the type is cast. The Linotype, and other machines based on the same principle, assembles a line of matrices, inserts adjustable space bars between the words, and then casts the whole line in type metal. The matrices, from which the cast or slug is made, are redistributed within the machine. Once the slug has been used it can be melted down and the metal used over again. This means the printing is always done from newly cast type metal. In addition to adjusting the line length to make all the lines even, the linecasting machine can also cast a slug which incorporates the spac-

The ABC's of Typography

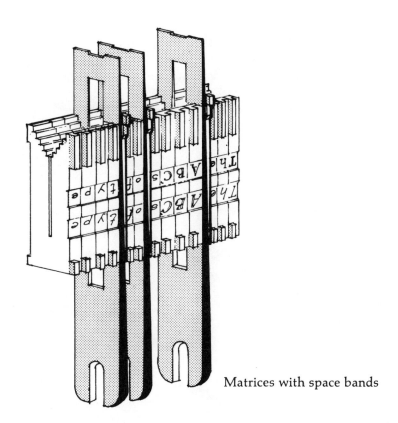

Matrices with space bands

ing between the lines, eliminating the need for placing thin pieces of metal (called leads) by hand between the lines. The Linotype and Intertype are two common linecasting machines used for body copy. The Ludlow is a linecasting machine which casts larger sizes of type for headlines and titles from hand-set matrices.

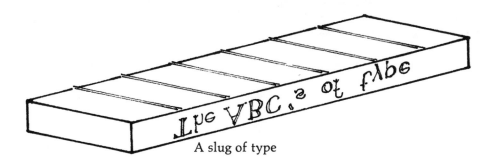

A slug of type

Strike-on Composition

Strike-on composition method is an outcome of two things: the revolution in office machines and the offset printing process. It's also called "direct-impression" composition because the "type" is set with equipment similar to the typewriter.

Since offset printing is basically a photographic process, anything that can be photographed can be used—including typewriter type. The common typewriter is a rather unsophisticated typesetting instrument. The typewriter companies have been improving the quality of the image so that now many of the machines produce an impression suitable for reproduction. The biggest problem with a typewriter is spacing between words and around letters. In a standard office typewriter, all letters, regardless of shape, occupy the same unit of space. That means there is a lot of air around an i while the m fills the unit completely. Some modern machines have variable spacing and variable-width letters which solve this problem somewhat.

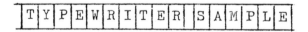

It is possible to achieve the look of justified copy using a typewriter by double typing. The line is typed up to the margin and the number of missing units noted. Then it is retyped with additional spacing between some words to make the line even with the margin.

A typeface which is to	+1	A typeface which is to
have anything like a	+3	have anything like a
present, let alone a	+3	present, let alone a
future, will be neither	0	future, will be neither
very "different" nor	+3	very "different" nor
very "jolly."		very "jolly."
--Stanley Morison		

The Justowriter and Varitype are more complicated systems which use punched tape and two typewriters to achieve the justified lines. With both of these systems the copy has to be typed twice, either by machine or by hand. The IBM composer is another type of strike-on typesetting equipment which is very popular because of the quality of its product and the ease of its use. These machines are used for body composition. They are ideal for in-office newsletters. While typographers live in fear of being replaced by secretaries, the quality of the strike-on systems is still below that of professional composition. The chief advantages are in cost and speed.

Computer and Phototypesetting

The technological revolution in typography took off in the 1960's with the combination of photographic principles and computers. In the past, authors, using typewriters and pencils, produced a revised manuscript that might be retyped by the author or by a secretary. The manuscript was sent to the compositor, where it was keyboarded all over again. Corrections were made by returning to the keyboard. Any one piece of copy might thus be keyboarded as many as five or six times. With computer equipment the manuscript need only be keyboarded once. The author may even type it directly onto punched or magnetic tape, using a typewriter keyboard. The tape can either be played out onto a piece of paper or projected onto a screen which resembles that of a television receiver. The actual final copy is set by a phototypesetting machine connected to the computer.

Proofreading can be done from the galley or from the screen and corrections entered into the tape. On the screen of the video display terminal the proofreader can watch while the errors disappear and are replaced with the corrected composition. When the proofreading is completed, the tape is corrected and fed into a computer, which plays out final copy, either ready for the camera in a reproduction proof or as a film that may be developed photographically.

The computer system speeds up the typesetting process by cutting down on the number of times the copy has to be keyboarded. Not only that, the copy can be stored on tape, which is far less cumbersome than the old-time metal and is particularly advantageous for large annual publications such as catalogs and directories. Errors become fewer because the copy is typed fewer times.

Both this computer/photosetting system and "strike-on" composition are called "cold type" in contrast to the hot-metal type discussed earlier. The computer methods are particularly versatile and limited only by our ability to write programming instructions. With the marriage of photography and computers, typography is seeing a new era of creativity. All

The ABC's of Typography

kinds of variations are possible through the optical systems of the camera. The sample photographic distortions shown here are used primarily for display. All of these were impossible to set with hot metal systems.

WAVY LINES
CURVES ARCS
SHADOW
BACKSLANT
STAGGER BACKWARDS

Western Typesetting

This is just a brief review of composition methods. From this range of systems you should be able to find a typesetting system to match the demands of your job.

Chapter 3

Type Measurement

Much to the dismay of some editors and artists, mathematics plays an important role in typography. The math is simple if you are familiar with the language of printers' measurements.

Printers in English-speaking countries measure type by the American or English point system. It was 200 years after Gutenberg invented movable type before the size of the metal pieces was finally standardized. During that period, foundries cast their type in whatever sizes they liked. There was no common way to talk about the size of type other than by pulling a proof and looking at it.

A point system was designed by a French printer, Fournier, in the 1700's, but it took a decree from King Louis XV before printers would use Fournier's points.

The American Point System

In the American point system, the height of the face of the type is stated in a very tiny unit called a point. There are approximately 72 points to an inch. One point equals .0138 inch, which is close enough to 1/72 inch for the kinds of calculations we will be doing.

72 points

1 inch

A line of type set in a 12-point size would be about 1/6 of an inch high.

1. *How big in inches is 36-point type?*   _____

   How many lines of 12-point type will fill a block of space 3 inches high?

                                                              _____

Picas. Since a point is so small, a larger unit is used to measure space. The *pica* is another basic measurement used by printers. As a matter of fact, the ruler that a printer uses is calibrated in picas and is frequently called a pica rule. It is also called a line gauge.

There are 12 points to a pica, hence 6 picas to an inch. You will become quite comfortable and familiar with picas because all type-using people use them and equipment is designed for them.

1 inch

6 picas

2. *A 3-inch column would be how wide in picas?*   _____

   How high in picas is a line of 12-point type?   _____

Ens and Ems. Printers measure the width of spaces in *ems*. This measure is used to indicate the size of paragraph indention and the spacing between words. The size of the em varies; it is dependent upon the size of the type you are using. An em is a square and it is as wide and as high as the size of the type. For example, the em in 12-point type is 12 points high and 12 points wide. In 6-point type the em is 6 points by 6 points. A related measure is the *en*, which is exactly ½ of the em in width. In 12-point type, the en is 6 points wide. Ems are sometimes called quads by printers.

☐How big   ☐☐How big

The ABC's of Typography

3. *With a line gauge, measure the height of the letters in How big.*
   How high is the line height in picas? In points? _____

   How wide in points is an em in that size type? _____

   How wide is an en in that type? _____

Ems are used most often to indicate indentions. A paragraph in a normal-width column would be indented one em. In an unusually wide column, two or three ems would be appropriate for the indention. This is particularly true if you are using an oversize initial letter or number to begin the paragraph.

[1] The genius of type designing
is the ability to give subtle
but pleasing modifications to
at least 26 overwhelmingly
ordinary geometric shapes,
designing them so they will
mesh harmoniously when
rearranged in different
combinations.
        --Edward Rondthaler

[3]   The genius of type designing is the ability to
give subtle but pleasing modifications to at least
26 overwhelmingly ordinary geometric shapes, designing
them so they will mesh harmoniously when rearranged
in different combinations.
        --Edward Rondthaler

4. *If you are setting 14-point type on a wide line and you decide you need*
   2½ times the normal indention, how many ems
   would you specify? _____

   Calculate how wide that indention would be in points. _____

   Convert that point width to picas. Approximately
   how many picas would the indention be? _____

Type sizes. Type ranges in size generally from 4 point to 144 point. Most typesetting machines only set up to 72 point. The common sizes are as follows:

    Classified-ad type: 5½ or 6
    Body Type: 8, 9, 10, 11, 12, 14
    Display Type: 18, 20, 24, 30, 36, 48, 60, 72
    Poster Type: 96, 120, 144 and above

"Agate" is a term used for the small type in newspapers, particularly in classified ads and legal notices. The term "body copy" is used to refer to the text in a book, magazine, ad, or newspaper. "Display" is another term for headlines and titles. "Poster" type is the extra-large sizes for such uses as posters, displays, and exhibits.

The Venus typeface on the next page is shown in a range of sizes from 12 to 96 point.

A word about type sizing: size is based on the metal body on which the letter is cast. For that reason the type impression or face does not measure exactly its stated size. The "shoulder" is that extra space on the face of the type body or slug which is not included in the typeface.

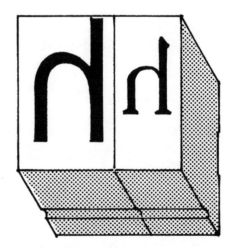

Some typefaces are "long on the body" and fill the slug. Other faces are "short on the body" and leave a lot of room on the shoulder. That's one reason two typefaces of the same stated size may appear to be different sizes.

The ABC's of Typography

12 **VEN**

18 **VEN**

24 **VEN**

30 **VEN**

36 **VEN**

42 **VEN**

48 **VEN**

54 **VEN**

60 **VEN**

72 **VEN**

96 **VEN**

Enlarging Type. The range of type sizes given here includes the common sizes for type set on typecasting machines. With the introduction of photography to typesetting, any face can now be set in any size, employing photographic enlargement and reduction. The constraints of the old metal molds no longer restrict the sizing of type. You will even find some printers photosetting type in such weird sizes as 9½ and 11½. However, an overenlarged typeface may not be true to its design. Type which comes from a typecasting machine is designed differently for the different sizes. In hot metal, the designer's goal is to make a face as easy to read in small sizes as it is in larger sizes. In order to do that, the proportions of the letter parts change slightly as the type size increases.

6 point type enlarged 12 times   72 point type as set

5. *Can you see two ways the 72-point letter design differs from the overenlarged 6-point letter?*

1. _____

2. _____

The Didot System

The American point system for measuring type is not universal. The point system designed by Fournier is international, but the size of the point used in Europe differs from the size of the English and American point. Fournier's system was modified to make the point fit the French inch and that change created what is known in Europe as the Didot system. In the Didot system a point equals 1.07 American points. In other words, the Didot point is larger than an American point.

Instead of using picas, European printers convert 12 didot points to a unit called a "cicero." For comparison, 14 ciceros equals approximately 15 picas.

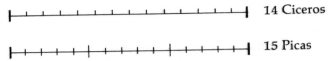

├───┼───┼───┼───┼───┼───┤ 14 Ciceros

├─┼─┼─┼─┼─┼─┼─┼─┼─┼─┼─┤ 15 Picas

Picas and ciceros differ just enough to prevent mixing type from one system with type from the other.

The Metric System

The difference between American and Didot points seems to be a moot issue since the metric system appears to be taking over the printing world. Printers and type founders have been using points for 300 years and they are not in a hurry to change to metric measures. But the American photo typesetting and the transfer-type companies are beginning to convert their type sizes to metric measures. Some newspapers have even started measuring columns in centimeters instead of in inches or agate lines.

25.3 mm
72 points
1 inch
6 picas

In almost exact measurement, 1 point equals .35 mm and 1 mm equals 2.85 points. Therefore 72 points (6 picas) equals approximately 25.24 mm (or 2.52 centimeters). You can nearly always figure that 6 picas and 1 inch are the same. Those are the basic relationships you need to remember. As the pica rule gives way to a metric rule, you won't need to make these mental conversions. Until that time, however, the table in Appendix 2 (page 172) will help you convert from points and picas to millimeters. As the measure in the American point system gets larger, we move from points to picas. In the metric system we would move from millimeters to centimeters (remember that 1 cm = 10 mm).

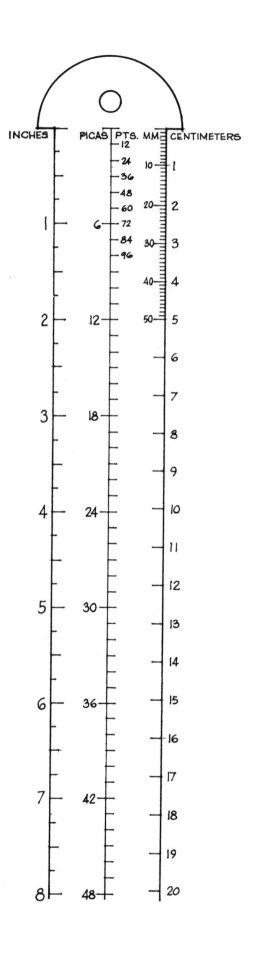

40

6. *Using the tables in the Appendix, find the equivalent size in millimeters of 60-point type.* _____

Convert that number to centimeters. _____
Calculate how big in millimeters 144-point type would be? _____

Convert that number to centimeters. _____
If you had a copy block that was 10 picas wide and 5 picas deep, what would the dimensions be in centimeters? _____

Review of Type Measurement

The American (or English) point system uses points and picas. The European Didot system uses points and ciceros. In the metric system type may be measured in millimeters and centimeters.

7. *You are setting up an ad and you have the choice of 10-point type or 12-point type.*
   Which size is the smaller? _____
8. *Suppose you decide to use the larger type in this ad.*
   How many lines would you get in a space 2 inches deep? _____

   In a space 8 centimeters deep? _____
9. *You are working with the 12-point type and your boss decides he wants to drop in the company's one-letter logo at the beginning of the copy. It measures 1 pica wide and 2 picas deep.*
   How many lines would be indented? _____

   How many ems would you indent the copy? _____
10. *You will be using two columns for the copy in this ad and you have a space 5 inches wide. Suppose you decide you want 4 picas between the columns.*
    How wide in picas would your columns be? _____

    Convert that column width to centimeters. _____

Chapter 4

Line, Word, and
Letter Spacing

Type designers are as much concerned with the amount of space between words, lines, and letters as they are with the face itself.

Spacing is functional. It separates units that need to be separated, like words. But the separations can set up patterns which become a visual distraction. Spacing can also guide the eye by setting up tracks to follow as the eye sweeps and scans the copy. This is a function of spacing between lines.

Spacing has an aesthetic purpose. Type that is compacted into a tight space becomes a dark mass visually. Type that is spread out over a space becomes a light mass. Sometimes this contrast serves a purpose, but usually the designer uses spacing to spread out the concentrated masses and pull together the light masses and thus even out the visual tone, which then makes the type easier to read.

Line Spacing

The amount of space around the lines of type may be as important to the designer as the size of the typeface. In the old days of hand-set type, a thin metal strip or lead (pronounced led) was inserted between the lines to space them out. Linecasting machines accomplished the same purpose by casting the type on a thick slug. For example, 12-point type on a 14-point slug provides 2 points of space between lines. With computer typesetting, leading is simply programmed as an instruction.

Leading is a concern primarily for body copy. Body copy, which is ordinarily set in 8 to 12-point sizes, will usually have one or two points of leading. The "line height" will thus be the size of the type plus the amount of the leading.

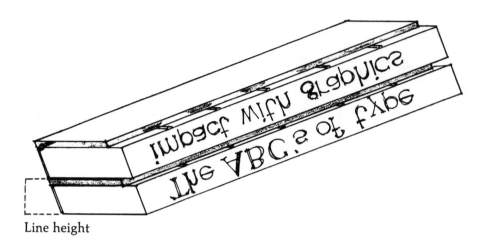

Line height

1. *If you are using 10-point type with 2 points leading,
    what is your line height?* _____

   *How many points would that line height make for six
    lines?* _____

   Convert that point figure for six lines to inches. _____

   Convert the same point figure into centimeters. _____

Either 10-point type with 2 points leading or 11-point type with 1 point leading equals one pica in depth. When copyfitting, this can simplify the computation since you are able to count lines on the basis that the number of lines equals the number of picas.

2. *Suppose you have a block for copy that is 6 inches deep. You are using
    10-point type and 2 points leading.*
   How many picas deep is the copy block? _____

   How many lines of copy will fit in that copy block? _____

The ABC's of Typography

Leading and Design. The amount of leading to be used between lines will usually vary with the design of the typeface. Faces that have big x-heights may need more space around the line than faces which have small x-heights and long ascenders and descenders. Compare the two type samples:

a. The classical idea that each letter has one perfect form is one which was tied at the Renaissance to the stone-cut monumental letter of the Romans. Perhaps if we detach it from this arbitrary connection it will still work today. It can surely be more logically applied to a sans serif letter based on objective geometrical principles.
—Nicolete Gray

b. The classical idea that each letter has one perfect form is one which was tied at the Renaissance to the stone-cut monumental letter of the Romans. Perhaps if we detach it from this arbitrary connection it will still work today. It can surely be more logically applied to a sans serif letter based on objective geometrical principles.
—Nicolete Gray

3. *Which face was set in 10-point with 1 point leading?* ——————

Which face was set in 10-point with 2 points leading? ——————

Another reason to vary the amount of leading is the length of the lines. The longer the lines the more space you need between them in order to help the reader's eye find its way back to the right place. Compare the type samples which follow:

The classical idea that each letter has one perfect form is one which was tied at the Renaissance to the stone-cut monumental letter of the Romans. Perhaps if we detach it from this arbitrary connection it will still work today. It can surely be more logically applied to a sans serif letter based on objective geometrical principles.

—Nicolete Gray

The classical idea that each letter has one perfect form is one which was tied at the Renaissance to the stone-cut monumental letter of the Romans. Perhaps if we detach it from this arbitrary connection it will still work today. It can surely be more logically applied to a sans serif letter based on objective geometrical principles.

—Nicolete Gray

4. *How many points of spacing would you say are between the lines in the short block?*

_____

How many points of spacing would you say are between the lines in the long block?

_____

Word Spacing

The amount of spacing between words will vary in typeset copy. This differs from a typewriter, which has a mechanical spacing unit that is the same throughout a copy block. Typeset spaces vary in order to make the edge of the column line up from line to line—this is called justifying the line. As a line is set mechanically, the typecasting machine inserts spacebands between the words. These spacebands are double wedges and they are adjusted until the line is the proper length.

In machine-justified copy the word spacing is the same throughout the line; different word spacing occurs only from line to line. There is a minimum and a maximum amount of space which can be inserted between words without disturbing the reading process. If the space is too little,

The difference between typesetting and typography is a
matter of aesthetics--the
difference between a purely
mechanical, mathematical
process and an art form.
                    --Paul D. Doebler

The difference between typesetting and typography is a matter
of aesthetics—the difference
between a purely mechanical,
mathematical process and an art
form.
                    —Paul D. Doebler

then the words will run together. If it is too much, the words separate until the eye has to stop and jump the gap between the words.

Spacing and Design. One of the biggest problems with word spacing comes with justified copy in a narrow column. Since there are few words in the line, the opportunities to space out the line are fewer. In some cases where a word can't easily be broken, the line may be so short of characters that the word spaces become holes. Sometimes the holes are so glaring they disrupt reading. When several lines are set with wide word spacing, the space between the words may line up and create up-and-down "rivers of white space" that can be as powerful optically as the horizontal movement along the line of type. Rivers and holes can usually be avoided by rewriting the copy slightly and by making the line length longer.

I am the voice of to-
day, the herald of to-
morrow . . . I coin for
you the enchanting tale,
the philosopher's mor-
alizing, and the poet's
visions . . . I am the
leaden army that con-
quers the world—I am
type.
                    —Frederic Goudy

Letter Spacing

In addition to spacing between lines and words, another concern is the spacing between letters, particularly in display copy. Generally the letter spacing from typesetting machines in body copy is satisfactory. The letter spacing from typewriters is not satisfactory, hence typographers and designers frown on typewriter-set copy. In contrast, computer typesetting is based on a module or grid which provides finer gradations in width for the letters. Most systems use 18-unit modules, but some are even finer, such as 36 or 54 units. The numerous resulting letter widths reduce the risk of unnecessary space between letters.

Display Type. Display type provides the real challenge with respect to letter spacing. When letters are big, then the amount of air around them becomes more obvious. Mechanically set display with an equal amount of space between all letters will probably need adjustment for some letter combinations.

5. *Study the display words, valve and between, and notice the patterns created by adjoining letter forms. Look for any pockets or holes of white space.*

VALVE

between

What pairs of letters seem to create distracting amounts of white space?

Another problem with display comes from the patterns created by combinations of letters. Certain letters stop the eye unless special care is taken in letter spacing. Remedying this fault may mean spacing out as well as spacing tight.

6. *Study the display words "schoolbook" and "hillbilly." Squint at them and look for overall patterns of light and dark masses.*

schoolbook

hillbilly

Can you see two general letter shapes that cause problems? Which are they?

1. _____

2. _____

The same two words are reset in the next example. To correct for the tall letters that appeared crowded, space was added. To correct for the round letters that appeared to spread, space was reduced.

schoolbook

hillbilly

7. *Between which letters was space added?* _____

Between which letters was less space used? _____

With display type it is important to space letters optically rather than mechanically. That means the spaces should *appear* to be the same. If spacing is mechanically set at a certain width, then some letters will appear to be closer together than others. This phenomenon results from the extreme vertical nature of some of our tall letters.

To correct for the optical density which results from massing tall letters, they need more space between them than the round letters need. Word spacing needs similar adjustment.

8. *In the display words in "little mammal," between which letters should more space be inserted?* _____

Between which letters should less space be used? _____

little mammal

Here is a suggestion for checking letter spacing; it helps focus on the spacing problem. Cover all the letters on both sides of three successive letters. The middle letter of the three should appear to be centered between the other two. When it so appears, there may actually be more space on one side than on the other, but optically the two outside letters are balanced against one another.

The purpose of letter spacing is to create textures of copy which are optically consistent by eliminating light and dark masses. Unadjusted groupings of tall vertical letter forms will appear dark and groupings of fat rounded letter forms will appear light. The principle is: use more space around vertical and less around rounded letters.

A similar rule applies to the size of the type. Copy that is set properly for display use appears much too tight when it is reduced. Body copy which is enlarged will seem to have too much space around the letters. The principle is: Use more space around letters in the smaller sizes and less space around those in the larger sizes.

Close Setting. Certain letter combinations just don't work very well together. Because of this, editors and designers may ask the typesetter to "underspace" or "set tight" these combinations. This is particularly true of letters which have sloping strokes and elements overhanging the stem. Observe the display word WATT. Notice how the space has been tightened around the A. It is called "kerning" when the space around the overhanging elements is tightened up.

WATT WATT

Letters can be set close by hand with transfer type. They can also be set close with many types of photo composition machines. Close setting is virtually impossible with linecasting equipment.

In photo composition, the spacing is calculated on 18 units to an em. (This may vary with the equipment.) For example, 1 unit in 18-point type would be 1 point wide. One unit in 36-point type would be 2 points wide. A counter totals the units in the line until the line is nearly full. The unfilled units are added to the word spacing to make the line justified.

 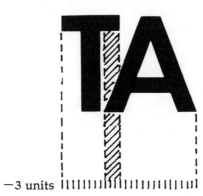

−3 units

In some machines it is also possible to include instructions about special unit spacing between the letters. Some even have a capability for "minus spacing." Regular spacing is considered zero, and the compositor can add or subtract up to three units.

+3 FAT LETTERSPACIN

+2 FAT LETTERSPACING

+1 FAT LETTERSPACING

0 FAT LETTERSPACING

−1 FAT LETTERSPACING

−2 FAT LETTERSPACING

−3 FAT LETTERSPACING

Close-set display type has some functional as well as aesthetic benefits. In big sizes, close-setting holds the word together visually. It also cuts down on the amount of spacing necessary between words.

Certain letter combinations need to be letter spaced regardless of close setting. A c and an o may be readable even when so close that they touch, but not an i or an l.

Tight:	−1	come	little
Touch:	−2	come	little
Lap:	−3	come	little

Review of Spacing

9. *You are designing an advertisement and you have the option of using either a 14-point line or a 30-point line. The type size is 10 point. Would you use 1 or 2 points leading with a 14-pica line?* _____

   Would you use 1 or 2 points leading with a 30-pica line? _____

10. *You have your choice between a typeface which has a big x-height and one with small x-height. Your copy block is 11 picas wide. Your line height must be 10 points.*

    Which style of type would you choose? _____

11. *You consider using 8-point type with 2 points leading. How many lines of type could be set in an inch-deep copy block?* _____

12. *The following title has been proposed for a book cover. Study the letter-form patterns. Draw circles where adjoining letters create "holes" of space. Draw a diagonal line between letters which seem to create dark masses.*

NEVER FAR FROM HILLY LAND

13. *The approved title for a book turns out to be a designer's nightmare.*

    Mark with a + those combinations of letters which need more than normal spacing. Mark with a — those letter combinations which need less than normal spacing.

An Overly Illustrated Balloon

Chapter 5

Type Identification

The preceding chapters have made numerous references to "typefaces." By now you probably realize that there are different kinds of type and that they look different from one another. Technically, the type's face is the impression area that carries the ink and that comes in contact with the paper in the press. However, when we refer to typeface, we will be talking about the distinctive "looks" of the letters in a particular design of type.

Typefaces

A person's face is distinctive, although certain elements are common to all human faces: eyes, mouth, nose. Your own face may be similar to other faces in your family, but there is no other face quite exactly like it. Typefaces are also distinctive. There are at least 5,000 different ones to choose from, and probably many more, given the capability of photography to copy and alter basic designs.

For communication with other artists, editors, and printers, it is helpful to be able to group or classify these typefaces in some way. We will use a system to classify type on four levels. We will start with what is called a *font*, then move to *series*, *families*, and *races* of typefaces.

Type Fonts

A font is a complete set or assortment of characters in one size and one typeface. It usually contains all of the upper and lower-case letters as well as punctuation marks, numerals, ligatures, and frequently used special characters.

AaBbCcDdEeFfGgHhIiJj
KkLlMmNnOoPpQqRrSs
TtUuVvWwXxYyZz
0123456789$!/&?;:-)(—[]#‡

A font of type

In the days when printers set type by hand, they stored all the individual characters of a type font in one case. When a printer spoke of a font, he meant everything in that one case. One case might have 8-point Cen-

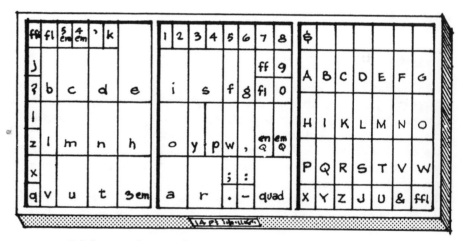

California job case showing location of letters in the font

tury Bold; another case would have 10-point Century Bold. The cases were stored in racks, like drawers. The font has always been basic in the typesetter's filing system. We still speak of fonts even though type is rarely handset. For hot-metal composition, a font is a set of matrices rather than a set of types. For photo composition, the strip or disk is equivalent to a font. A font of transfer type may fill one or several sheets.

The ABC's of Typography

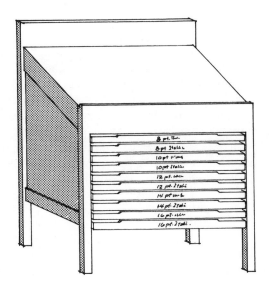

Type Series

When typesetters speak of the series they have available in a certain face, they mean the sizes they have. For example, a printer might have fonts of 8- and 10-point for body copy and 24-, 36-, and 48-point for display, then his series would be 8-, 10-, 24-, 36-, and 48-point.

One advantage of photo composition is that it virtually eliminates restrictions of series. If the compositor has a strip or disk for any one face, he can usually use it to set this face in several sizes. Systems differ in this respect; some use separate strips for body and display. None, however, need a separate strip for each size in the series.

Type Families

Families of type contain all the size series and the style variations of a common face. For example, the Cheltenham family contains at least 16 different faces. The Caslon family includes at least 15. Spartan and Univers have as many as 27 variations. With photographic techniques, a single face may have as many as 60 variations.

Three kinds of style variations are based on width, weight, and posture. Because of these built-in variations, you can design a printed piece and have a variety of choices while still maintaining unity of type design.

	Univers Roman	Univers Italic
Light	ABCDEF	ABCDEF
Medium	ABCDEF	ABCDEF
Demi Bold	**ABCDEF**	**ABCDEF**
Bold	**ABCDE**	**ABCDE**

Condensed

Light	ABCDEFGHI	ABCDEFGHI
Medium	ABCDEFGHI	ABCDEFGHI
Demi	**ABCDEFG**	**ABCDEFG**

Expanded

Light	ABCDEF	ABCDEFGH
Medium	**ABCDE**	ABCDEFGH
Demi	**ABCDE**	**ABCDEFG**

Width. The width of a type style refers to the amount of horizontal space the letters cover. One face within a family may be skinny. We call that condensed. A fat face may be called extended, expanded, or wide. The width in the middle normally does not carry a width designation. We will call it medium in our comparisons here. Look at this sample of three alphabets. Notice the differences in the c and the h.

condensed
abcdefghijklmnopqrstuvwxyz

medium
abcdefghijklmnopqrstuvwxyz

extended
abcdefghijklmnopqrstu

1. *Letter your name in both condensed and extended letters.*

_____

_____

_____

_____

_____

Some faces may have highly exaggerated variations in their width. They may be ultra-expanded or ultra-condensed. Usually their names will indicate these.

Gill Ultra Bold

2. *In this list, which faces are condensed? Mark them C.*
Which faces are extended? Mark them X.

1. __ **FOLio**

2. __ **CLArendon**

3. __ **placard**

4. __ **MICROGRAMMA**

5. __ **Grotesk**

6. __ **CLArendon**

7. __ **NEWS GOTHIC**

8. __ Roman

3. *Suppose you have been asked to design a new magazine. You want all your display section heads to fit into one column in a two-column page. What width face would you look for?*

— Extended   — Condensed

4. *You are trying to fit a brief title for an article across a double-page spread.*
What width face would you look for?

— Extended   — Condensed

Weight. Another way to describe the individual faces within a type family is by their weight. Type of any size can vary in weight. Type weights are usually identified as light, medium, and bold or heavy.

Tiffany Light
Tiffany Medium
Tiffany Demi
Tiffany Heavy

Note that the weight of the face is not necessarily a function of its width. Bold, extended typefaces are numerous but faces in the same family may be light extended or bold condensed. Width and weight are two independent design features. The weight is determined by the thickness of the strokes, not by the size of the letter.

Study the variations between light and bold in the lower-case alphabets of the Avant Garde family.

light
abcdefghijklmnopqrstuvwxyz
bold
abcdefghijklmnopqrstuvwx

The ABC's of Typography

5. *Letter your name in both light and bold weights.*

6. *Study the list of typefaces.*

1 Serif Gothic   5 Arthur

2 **Avant Garde**   6 **Tiffany**

3 Univers   7 Avant Garde

4 Tiffany   8 Serif Gothic

Which faces represent bold designs?

_____

Which faces represent light designs?

_____

Posture. A third way that typefaces can vary is with respect to posture or slant. Aside from ornamental faces and scripts, most families have a variation that slants to the right and is called italic. These letters slant, but do not connect as some of the cursive or script styles do. The cursives are imitation handwriting, but the italics maintain the design of the upright letter.

Souvenir Italic
Murray Hill

In the Sixteenth century, italic was a family all its own. Since then the term has been used to refer to a variation in posture, rather than to a distinctive typeface. A more appropriate term for this slanted variation is "oblique." Occasionally this term is used but it has never become general, so we still use the word *italic*

The upright version of a letter is called roman. This, too, is confusing because the term *roman* is used also to identify a design style. Whenever you see the term *roman*, your first problem is to decide whether it refers to a style of type or to the upright variation.

1 *Murray Hill*   5 SERIF GOTHIC

2 PALADIUM   6 *Century*

3 **Univers**   7 MIStral

4 *Commercial*

7. *In the type samples here identify all the italic faces.*

Just as weight and width are independent variations, so is posture. An italic can be condensed or extended, bold and light. Most typefaces will therefore be identified as to all three variations, such as "Caslon bold condensed italic" or "Futura light extended." Unless one of the variations is specified, the compositor will assume that the medium roman is wanted. For example, "Bodoni condensed" with nothing said about weight will get set in a medium weight. The roman posture will always be set unless italic is specified.

The ABC's of Typography

Review of Type Families

You can see what a tremendous number of options are available within any one type family because of these basic variations.

8. *In the outline below, list the three major style variations with their categories.*

    1. _____
       a. _____
       b. _____
       c. _____
    2. _____
       a. _____
       b. _____
       c. _____
    3. _____
       a. _____
       b. _____

9. *Study the assortment of typefaces in the group shown here. Identify by number:*

1. AVANT GARDE
2. Dashow
3. **Franklin Gold**
4. **AVANT GARDE**
5. *Murray Hill*
6. PALADIUM
7. **Souvenir**
8. **Primus**
9. **Franklin**
10. King Arthur
11. **TIFFANY**
12. *Palace*

The condensed faces _____
The extended faces _____
The italic faces _____
The bold faces _____
The light faces _____

Type Races

When used to identify typefaces, *race* refers to some common characteristic that applies to a number of type families as a group. Type classification by race is the broadest system of categories and the least well-defined. Printers do not agree among themselves on how many races there are. They don't even use the same names. The following lists give an example of the classifications used in two typesetting specification books:

Book A	Book B
Old Styles	Scripts
Transitionals	Gothics
Modern Romans	Spartans
Sans Serifs	Bodonis
Square Serifs	Square Serifs
	Moderns

Obviously there aren't many points of agreement between the two. For our discussion here we will use six categories. The first three are faces for special moods and uses. The last three contain the basic everyday body and display faces.

Black Letters
Scripts and Cursives
Ornamentals
Romans
Sans Serifs
Contemporary Serifs

We will begin our discussion of these type races by looking first at the special use categories.

Black Letters

The type race we are calling black letter goes under a number of different names. You may hear it referred to as Old English, gothic, or text letters. While the term *Old English* is commonly used, we avoid it here because many of the faces are in fact German. We also avoid *gothic;* in the United States it sometimes refers to sans serif faces.

The black-letter faces reproduce the styles of hand lettering popular in much of Europe at Gutenberg's time. Their predominant characteristics in-

clude heavy vertical strokes, angles, and delicate hairlines for ornamentation. These letters are used for formal occasions such as diplomas and invitations. They establish the feeling of a monumental event. They are sometimes used for ads and books where the subject is history or antiquity.

Scripts and Cursives

Scripts and cursives are also used for formal occasions. They are patterned after fine penmanship and frequently are ornamented with flourishes. Letters in this race are usually highly rounded, slant to the right, and either connect from letter to letter or have a tail on the letter which leads to the next.

Scripts are sometimes confused with italics because both types of letters slant. Italic letters are not imitations of cursive or running handwriting. They may slant but the nature of the letter remains true to its family. Neither do the italic letters connect or maintain the tail stroke at the end of the letter which suggests a connection.

ABCDEFGHIJKLM
NOPQRSTUVWXYZ
abcdefghijklmnopqrstuvwxyz

Ornamentals

The classification we call ornamentals is also known as novelty faces. This type race contains an assortment of faces which are not related visually, but functionally.

Mood. One kind of ornamental typeface is highly emotive. It seeks to create a mood. Some samples of these faces are included here.

PORKY

FLINTSTONE

MANDARIN SHADED

FRANKENSTEIN'S BRIDE

Breakaway

MISS KITTY

Imitative. Another kind of ornamental face is designed to represent something else: computer print outs, baseball bats, balloons. Some look like they are hand-lettered and many of these are available through photo composition or transfer type.

ALDERWOOD

DRACULA

VAMPIRE

FIREBALL

IGLOO

Fortune Stencil

IGLOO OUTLINE

MOORE LIBERTY

10. *Pick an ornamental face and letter your name in that style.*

_____

_____

_____

_____

_____

_____

Romans

The roman category is probably the largest group of typefaces. Many of these faces were designed between 1500 and 1700 in the early days of typesetting.

The roman faces were the first faces designed specifically for printing instead of for hand-lettering. They are different in several respects from the highly ornamented calligraphy and black-letter faces of the Middle Ages.

The biggest difference is size. Type letters are smaller than hand-lettered shapes, hence cannot support as much ornamentation. In the days of the hand-lettered manuscripts, the scribes tried to make the letters as uniform as possible. In small printed letters, the type designers try to make the individual letters as recognizable as possible, despite the stylistic unity of the typeface design. Basically, printed roman letters are simpler than their hand-lettered predecessors—and much easier to read.

It is hard to say for sure when the first of anything happened, however, most typographers credit Nicholas Jenson with the development of the first roman type in or around 1470. Cloister Old Style is an accurate reproduction of Jenson's design. Claude Garamond in 1542, John Baskerville and William Caslon in the early 1700's, are three other big names in the design of roman faces. To this day, we still use Caslon, Garamond, and Baskerville typefaces even though the typeface designs may be as many as 300 years old.

The term roman may cause some confusion since it is also used to refer to the upright letter as opposed to a slanted italic letter. The printing industry will probably continue double use of this term. It's not a serious problem, since the context usually makes clear whether the meaning is roman/italic or the type race roman.

Within the roman type race, there are not only numerous faces but also some distinct variations. It takes a discriminating and sensitive eye to see the differences, but they are important differences to professional designers and editors. We will divide the roman race into three categories:

Old Style   Transitional   Modern

Old Style and Modern. Old-style and modern romans are quite different in slant, stroke, and treatment of the serif; transitional romans combine characteristics of both. When we use the term *modern*, we are speaking of a face from a design standpoint rather than from its age. For example, Bodoni, the classic modern roman, was designed by Giambattista Bodoni about the time of the American Revolution. It is a contemporary of Caslon in time, but not in style. On the other hand, Goudy Old Style was designed by Frederic Goudy in the 1930's. In the examples here we will use Garamond as a typical old-style roman and Bodoni as a modern roman. Study the two capital alphabets and see if you can see any difference.

ABCDEFGHIJKLMN
OPQRSTUVWXYZ

Garamond

ABCDEFGHIJKLMN
OPQRSTUVWXYZ

Bodoni

The most obvious difference between old-style and modern faces is in the serifs. In modern faces, the serifs are straight, flat, and vertical or horizontal. In old-style romans, the serifs are inclined and curve into the stroke. Printers say these serifs are bracketed to the stem.

Another difference is seen in the strokes. Study the word *do* in old-style and modern romans.

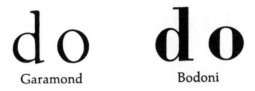

As you can see there is much more contrast between thick and thin strokes in the modern roman than there is in the old-style roman. The obvious distinction between thick and thin is a prominent characteristic of the modern romans.

Another distinction between modern and old style is in the stress of the stroke and the slant of the loops. This characteristic is a little more difficult to analyze.

11. *Draw an upper case E, H, T and W in both Garamond and Bodoni.*

You can easily see that Bodoni is highly vertical. It's straight up and down—almost rigid. Garamond tends to slant its loops. The thin strokes fall on the upper left and lower right. If you try writing a loop letter with a broad-point pen, you will find that the slant and diagonal stress are a natural result of the way a right-handed person would form the loop using two strokes. The modern romans are mechanically formed with a strong vertical stress.

abcdefghijklmnopqrstuvwxyz
Garamond

abcdefghijklmnopqrstuvwx
Bodoni

12. *Make an o with a broad-point marker. Use two strokes and notice what happens to the thicks and thins.*

13. *Draw a lower-case e and an upper-case c in both Garamond and Bodoni. Now go back and draw a line diagonally between the thick strokes of the loop. Which direction does the line slant?*

14. *Draw a lower case d and an upper case m in both Garamond and Bodoni and emphasize stress and slant patterns and the contrast in thick and thins.*

The ABC's of Typography

Transitional. The transitional faces are basically old styles; however, their designers have made obvious attempts to adopt the features of the modern romans. Century Schoolbook is a good example. Compare it with Garamond and Bodoni which we discussed previously.

ABCDEFGHIJKLMNO PQRSTUVWXYZ
abcdefghijklmnopqrstuvwxyz

With Century Schoolbook, the serifs are becoming more perpendicular; the thick and thins are more prominent, and the slant is less obvious than with Goudy Old Style.

15. *Draw a lower-case a and g and an upper case B and Z in old style, transitional, and modern roman styles.*

You will find the more common roman faces grouped here in the three categories of old style, transitional and modern.

Old Style

Garamond

CASlon

Cheltenham

Goudy

Plantin

Tiffany

Transitional

Baskerville

Times Roman

Century Schoolbook

CALIFORNIA

Palladium

Modern

BODoni Bold

Modern

The ABC's of Typography

You will note that one typeface above is identified as California. This is a name used by one type manufacturer for a face which is more commonly known as Caledonia. The typeface Palladium is an adaptation of the face by Herman Zapf called Palatino. In the appendix (page 185) you will find a list of some of these alternative names for similar type designs.

16. *Here are a number of type specimens. See if you can discriminate between the three groups.*

1 abcdefghijklmnopqrstuvwxyz

2 ABCDEFGHIJKLMNOPQRSTUV

3 ABCDEFGHIJKLMNOPQRST

4 abcdefghijklmnopqrstuvwxyz

5 ABCDEFGHIJKLMNOPQRSTUVWXYZ

6 abcdefghijklmnopqrstuvwxyz

7 ABCDEFGHIJKLMNOPQRST

8 abcdefghijklmnopqrstuvwxyz

9 ABCDEFGHIJKLMNOPQRST

10 abcdefghijklmnopqrstuvwxyz

Which faces are old style? _____

Which faces are transitional? _____

Which are modern romans? _____

Sans Serifs

The fifth major group of typefaces is called sans serif. Obviously the major distinction between this face and the romans has to do with the serif.

M M

To designers who love the roman faces, the sans serif letters are misshapen and ugly. These designers feel that the very elements which give grace and beauty to typefaces are the features which were dropped from the design of the sans serifs. (Some English typographers call the sans serifs by the name *grotesque*. In the United States, one name for them has been *gothic*, but that is to be avoided since in Europe it signifies the black letters.) Most sans serif faces are formed with uniform, unshaded strokes.

We show a selection here of seven common sans serif faces.

News Gothic Condensed
Helvetica
FUTURA BOLD
AVANT GARDE
UNIVERS
FOLIO MEDIUM EXTENDED
MICROGRAMMA BOLD EXT

The ABC's of Typography

The sans serif typefaces were much favored by the functionalists of the Bauhaus school of design in the 1920's. This design approach glorifies function over ornamentation. It represents the machine age—essentially technologic, unadorned, and mathematically determined. The Bauhaus school contributed to the design of furniture, skyscrapers, and hundreds of industrial products. The sans serif letter is to the skyscraper as the hand-lettered face of medieval manuscripts is to the cathedral. Every age has its own design form and it transcends artistic categories.

17. *Study this assortment of typefaces. Identify the sans serifs by number.*

---

1 abcdefghijklmnopqrstuvwxyz
2 abcdefghijklmnopqrstuvwx
3 **ABCDEFGHIJKLMNOPQRST**
4 ABCDEFGHIJKLMNOPQRST
5 ABCDEFGHIJKLMNOPQRST
6 ABCDEFGHIJKLMNOPQRSTU
7 abcdefghijklmnopqrstuvwxy

Contemporary Serifs

Recent years have seen the design of a number of essentially uniform-stroke faces with square or round serifs. Because of the serif they can't be classified as "sans serif." Because of the uniform, sometimes blocky strokes, they can't be called roman. These faces are increasing in popularity. It seems to be time to establish them as a category of their own. There are three basic kinds of type in this category: square serifs, round serifs, and inscribed serifs.

Square Serifs. The square-serif letter was popular first as a poster letter in the late 1800's. It was an imitation of the square stencil-type letters used on the big circus posters of that day. The square-serif letters are basically uniform-stroke in style and have a heavy slab serif with no bracketing.

The 1930's found a resurgence of this design in a face by Rudolph Weiss called Memphis. Perhaps these letters reminded artists of Egyptian design elements. At any rate, some of the square-serif typefaces are named after that period—Egyptian, Karnak, and Cairo for example. Other names are Stymie, Playbill, and Craw Clarendon.

CLARENDON
Lubalin Graph

18. *Letter your name in a square-serif style.*

abcdeefghijklmnopqrsttuvwxyz

The ABC's of Typography

Round Serifs. Typefaces with rounded serifs represent an amalgamation of styles. They use the basic rounded shape of the romans and the serifs are heavy and round.

Cooper Black is the most famous style with rounded serifs. Souvenir, a more recently designed round-serif face, comes in a variety of weights.

Cooper Black
Son of Windsor
Souvenir Bold
Clearface

19. *Using Cooper Black as a pattern, letter your name in a round-serif style.*

abcdefghijklmnopqrstuvwxyz

Inscribed Serifs. Letters with inscribed serifs are basically sans serif except they have a small widening at the base of the letter and the stems to sug-

E

gest a serif. This is a subtle chisel effect. Another variation of this letter is found on some faces which are basically sans serif but have small serifs on only a few letters. Here are some examples of inscribed-serif faces:

Threadgill
Perpetua
Korinna

Baker Danmark 1
Americana
Newtext Regular
SERIF GOTHIC

20. *Using Serif Gothic as a pattern, letter your name in an inscribed serif type style.*

ABCDEFGHIJKLMNOPQRSTUVWXYZ
abcdefghijklmnopqrstuvwxyz

The ABC's of Typography

21. *In the assortment of ten type-specimen alphabets, identify the type of serifs.*

1 abcdefghijklmnopqrstuvwxy

2 **ABCDEFGHIJKLMNOPQRSTUVWXYZ**

3 ABCDEFGHIJKLMNOPQRSTUVWXYZ

4 abcdefghijklmnopqrstuvwxyz

5 ABCDEFGHIJKLMNOPQRSTUV

6 **ABCDEFGHIJKLMNOPQRSTUVWXYZ**

7 abcdefghijklmnopqrstuvwxyz

8 ABCDEFGHIJKLMNOPQRSTUVWXYZ

9 **abcdefghijklmnopqrstuvwxyz**

10 **ABCDEFGHIJKLMNOPQRSTUVWXYZ**

Which faces have square serifs? ——————————

Which have round serifs? ——————————

Which have inscribed serifs? ——————————

Review of Type Races

We have discussed six different type races. Some of them are broken down into categories and some not. For a review of these groups, complete this outline of the type races:

22. 1. _____

    2. _____

    3. _____

       a. _____

       b. _____

    4. _____

       a. _____

       b. _____

       c. _____

    5. _____

    6. _____

       a. _____

       b. _____

       c. _____

The ABC's of Typography

23. *See how many typefaces you can identify by type race in the conglomeration of twelve alphabets.*

1 **abcdefghijklmnopqrstuvwxyz**

2 abcdefghijklmnopqrstuvwxyz

3 *abcdefghijklmnopqrstuvwxyz*

4 **abcdefghijklmnopqrstuvwxyz**

5 **abcdefghijklmnopqrstuvwxyz**

6 **ABCDEFGHIJKLMNOPQRSTUVWXYZ**

7 *abcdefghijklmnopqrstuvwxyz*

8 abcdefghijklmnopqrstuvwxyz

9 ABCDEFGHIJKLMNOPQRSTUVWX

10 **ABCDEFGHIJKLMNOPQRSTUVWXYZ**

11 abcdefghijklmnopqrstuvwxy

12 **abcdefghijklmnopqrstuvwxy**

Scripts _____

Sans serifs _____

Old-style romans _____

Ornamentals _____

Round serifs _____

Modern romans _____

Black letters _____

Transitional romans _____

Square serifs _____

Inscribed serifs _____

Chapter 6

Copyfitting

The editor of *Communication Arts* magazine has estimated in an editorial that the editing and design professions spend some $1 million daily to pay for editorial changes in type. Some of these changes are forced by updating information and making necessary corrections. But much of this expense is a product of sloppy editing. The most expensive and the most needless change is to reset copy because it doesn't fit.

Copyfitting is the process of trying to figure out, before the copy is sent to the printer, how long the copy is and how much space it will fill. It is a complicated art because so many things can vary: the size of the manuscript, the size of the type you use, and the amount of space available for the type.

It's analogous to trying to design a patio. The shape and amount of space covered by the patio can vary. The size of the individual paving stones can vary. Likewise the number of paving stones you have available can vary.

But the biggest headache in copyfitting—as in planning a patio—is that you can't just count things: you have to estimate. With a patio you have to estimate the approximate number of paving stones. You have to estimate the average size of the stones, and you will probably have to estimate the size of the space you have in mind for the patio.

Let's say you have a truck load of paving stones and you want to know how much space they will cover. You're probably not going to unload the truck and count them one by one. Instead you estimate how many are in the load by estimating how many will cover the floor of the truck bed and then multiply that by an estimate of how many layers of stones there are in the load.

But that only solves half the problem. The paving stones aren't all the same size so you also have to estimate the average size. By multiplying the number of stones you estimated to be in the load by the estimated average size of the stones, you would have some idea how much space the truck load will cover.

But you may want to approach the patio problem from a different angle. If you have picked the location and staked out the shape of the patio, then you may want to begin by estimating how big the patio will be. You measure width and depth (plus or minus such extras as steps, fountains, and open space where you might go around a tree) and from this you estimate the size of the patio.

The "fitting" part of the problem occurs when you bring the truck load of stones to the space in your backyard. You may find you have enough stones to cover the whole back yard—or the opposite may be true: you've marked off a patio that would take two truckloads to fill. But if you carefully estimate both stones and patio space ahead of time, then you should be able to tell if the truck load will cover a space similar in size to your planned patio.

What this patio story illustrates is that there are two ways to approach the copyfitting problem.

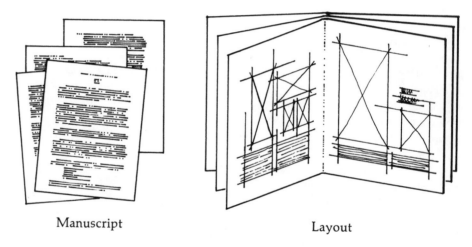

Manuscript   Layout

The designer or layout artist may have to estimate the length of a manuscript before beginning to develop the layout. On the other hand the editor or copywriter may receive a layout with a copy block indicated by a ruled box. The challenge is to write copy to fit that space.

Whichever the approach, the first step is to estimate. If the amount of space is fixed, then you have to estimate the amount of copy—in other words, write the copy to fit the space. If the copy is written, then you have to estimate the amount of space—design the space to fit the copy.

Characters-Per-Pica

Before we go through either of these methods step by step, let's first talk about the CPP or characters-per-pica. This is an index which printers use to compare the width of typefaces. You should remember from our earlier discussion that typefaces can vary in width even though they may be the same size. For example, with one face you may be able to get 1½ average-size characters in a single pica. With another face of the same point size, you may be able to get three average-size characters in a pica. When we actually compute the characters per pica, we use a typical line of type, count the characters and divide by the width (in picas) of the line measure. That gives us an index which is called CPP or characters-per-pica.

To give you an idea of how much type width can differ, consider 8-point Century Schoolbook which has a CPP of 2.89. This means an average of 2.89 characters will fit into one pica. In contrast, 8-point Univers Light has a CPP of 3.16.

1. *In a type line of the same length, will 8-point Century Schoolbook or 8-point Univers Light have the greater number of characters?*

   _____

   How many characters of 8-point Univers Light will fit into a 10-pica line?

   _____

   How many characters of 8-point Century Schoolbook will fit into a 10-pica line?

   _____

Note that the type with the smaller CPP is the wider typeface. It takes up more space proportionately than the face with the large CPP.

You usually don't have to compute the CPP for every face you use. Your printer's type specimen book should contain the CPP for the various faces in their common sizes. If that information isn't available from your printer, then you may look it up in a reference. Most books on graphic production contain a list of character counts for common faces. Another good source is the *Art Director's Copyfitter* which is available from Art Direction Book Company. An abbreviated list adapted from the *AD Copyfitter* is given in Appendix 3 of this book (page 174).

2. *In the CPP chart in the Appendix look up the character count for the following faces:*

8-point Avant Garde Med. Cond.   _____

8-point Cooper Black   _____

12-point Tiffany Heavy   _____

12-point Garamond Italic   _____

If for some reason you can't look up the CPP and you need to estimate it yourself you can do it by asking your printer to set a sample paragraph or the lowercase alphabet in the size and typeface you want to use. Count the number of characters in several lines and figure the average character count. Divide that by the line length, and you will have an estimate of the CPP for that face.

Please note that there is a lot of variation in CPP calculation because of phototypesetting. You need to know the machine the type will be set on in order to have any kind of reliable CPP estimates.

3. *Compute your estimate of the character count for the typeface used in the following paragraph.*

> completed graduate courses at other accredited
> institutions may transfer up to ten credit hours
> provided the courses are related and can be in-

What is the average number of characters counted in the three lines?

_____

What does the line width measure in picas?   _____

Divide the average character count by the line length you measured and what do you compute for the CPP?

_____

Once you understand the CPP concept, and know how to find it, you're ready to begin copyfitting.

Making the Space Fit the Copy

Let us first look at the approach where the copyfitting responsibility lies with the designer. The copy has already been written and the designer or artist has to design a layout for that amount of type. This is the method most frequently used with magazine layouts.

There are two steps in the process. First you need to figure how many lines of typeset copy the manuscript will set. The second step is to convert that number of lines to picas so that you can actually measure it on the layout.

Let's begin with the manuscript. For this discussion we'll assume the manuscript is just one page long. Your objective is to estimate how long that typewritten manuscript will be when it is typeset. You know already that typeset copy will probably be a different size from typewriter copy.

In order to make that conversion from typewriter to typeset, you need two pieces of information: the total number of characters in the manuscript and the number of characters in one line of the typeset copy.

Manuscript Characters. To find the number of characters in your manuscript, count them. (Remember that a space between the words is a character.) You may estimate the total number of characters by counting several lines and finding the average count—then multiply that total times the number of lines.

Typeset Characters. To find the number of characters in a line of typeset copy, you need to know or decide the type specificatons. This would include: the type, its size, and the line length.

Specifications:
10 pt. Bodoni
2 pts. Leading
13 pica line

The first piece of information you need is the CPP for the specified type face. You may find it using any of the methods discussed previously. Once you have the CPP then you multiply that times the specified line length which gives you the estimated number of characters in a line. For example if the CPP is 3.1 and your specifications call for a 20 pica line, then the total number of characters in a line would be 62.

4. *What is the CPP for 10-point Garamond Italic?* _____

Using that CPP, compute how many characters will go into a 24-pica line. _____

Fitting Manuscript Copy to Typeset Specifications. Your objective, remember, is to convert the manuscript to typeset copy. You have computed the total number of characters in the manuscript. Now divide that by the number of characters in one line of typeset copy and you will have an estimate of the number of typeset lines. The "fitting" process looks like this:

$$\left\{ \begin{array}{l} \text{Total} \\ \text{Manuscript} \\ \text{Characters} \end{array} \right\} \text{divided by} \left\{ \begin{array}{l} \text{Characters} \\ \text{in Typeset} \\ \text{Line} \end{array} \right\} \text{equals} \left\{ \begin{array}{l} \text{Number of} \\ \text{Typeset} \\ \text{Lines} \end{array} \right\}$$

5. *From Appendix 2, what is the CPP of 12-point Newtext?*

Using this CPP how many characters would fit in a 18-pica line? _____

If a manuscript has a total of 1,554 characters, how many 18-pica lines would that set in 12-point Newtext? _____

That was the first step and it gives you an estimate of how many lines long the manuscript will be when it's set in type. The second step is to convert that number of lines to something that you can measure on a layout. You can't measure by "number of lines," you need the number converted to some linear measure like picas, inches, or centimeters.

The process is fairly simple. You need to know the line height, which is the total number of points in the type size plus the leading. The line height is multiplied times the number of lines to get the total number of points in the copy block. For example, if you are using 8-point type with 2 points leading, your line height would be 10 points. That height times the number of lines, equals the total number of points. Let's say for illustration we have calculated 18 lines. In this case the total depth of the copy block would be 180 points. Since it's hard to measure points, you will probably want to convert that back to picas by dividing the total points by 12. So in this case, the 18 lines of 10-point type with 2 points leading would measure 15 picas in depth. That entire calculation is summarized here in numbers:

$$\frac{10 \times 18}{12} = 15$$

I might point out one shortcut. If you are using a type that has a total line height of 12 points, then the conversion is greatly simplified. If you changed the 10-point line height in the equation to 12 points, then you would be able to cancel the two 12's. In other words, if your line height equals 12 points, then it also equals one pica. That means your number of lines will equal the number of picas. With 12-point type height, 18 lines automatically will measure 18 picas.

6. *If you are setting 24 lines of type in 11 on 12 Bodoni,*
   how deep will the copy block be in picas?   _____

   How deep in inches?   _____
   How many picas deep will 24 lines be when set in 8
   on 9 Cairo?   _____

Review

Now you have converted the manuscript to typeset characters and calculated how many lines long the typeset copy block will be. Finally you converted that number of lines to picas. You are ready to begin your layout. You can mark on the dummy page exactly how much space the manuscript copy will occupy.

Shortcuts. After you become proficient with this method or at least understand the steps, you might benefit by using some of the following shortcuts.

1. Character Count Estimator—In Appendix 4 (page 178) you will find a character-count estimator which is adapted from the plastic scale which comes with the AD Copyfitter. This chart lets you look up the character-per-line information which you calculated previously by multiplying. All you need is the CPP and the length of the line of type. The left-hand column of this chart has CPP numbers from .80 to 6.01; the top and bottom of both pages of the chart have a pica scale.

Along the side, you locate the CPP figure for your typeface. Then you follow the line across from the CPP figure until you come to the pica number which represents the length of your line. Where these lines intersect you can read the character count for a line of type with that CPP.

7. *Look up the CPP for 10-point Caslon Old Face in Appendix 3.* _____

   Turn to Appendix 3 and find that CPP, Read across to the character count for an 18-pica line. What did you find? _____

2. Long Manuscript—If you have manuscript copy that is several pages long, such as the typewriter manuscript on the next page, you may not want to count the total number of characters for the entire manuscript.

An easy way to avoid calculating total characters is to figure the number of characters in a manuscript line and estimate typeset lines for each page. Count off the number of characters in a typeset line on the manuscript. Draw a vertical pencil line down the manuscript to mark off this portion of all the lines. That line represents the length of your typeset column. The left-over portion to the right of the vertical line will make less than one line of type. Find an average length line and count the total number of left-over characters to the right of your pencil line. By comparing that with your characters-per-line, you can figure what proportion of a line that left-over section represents.

For example let's say you have 41 characters in a typeset line and you draw a vertical pencil line at that point on the manuscript. You then count an average of 30 characters in the left-over line which is ¾ of the line length. That means every four left-over lines would equal three full lines.

Now you can just count the number of full lines and the pieces and you have come up with an estimated number of lines without having to multiply and calculate total character counts. This method is not as reliable as total characters, but it is fast and saves on calculations when you're working with a long manuscript.

3. Typewriter Scale—On the top and bottom of the chart in Appendix 4 you will find two scales. One is for an elite typewriter and the other is for a pica. By linking up the appropriate scale with the manuscript characters, you can read the number of characters in the line. This just

The ABC's of Typography

Explanations$_{T,F,D}$ are the notions which best summarize instrumental or instructional communication. Explanation$_T$ summarizes the teaching process: Somebody explains something to someone. In contrast Explanations$_{F,D}$ are product oriented. The distinction here is the difference between an explanation (product) and to explain (process). Since this study will be investigating explanatory messages which are products of a shared communication situation, the two explanatory notions to be evaluated in this study are Explanation$_F$ and Explanation$_D$. The distinction between these two explanations is the role of the source and receiver. Explanation$_F$ is source-oriented and Explanation$_D$ is receiver oriented. The difference between the two is analogous to talking to and talking with someone. When the source "talks to" someone, the receiver is passive and non-involved. When the source talks "with" someone, the receiver is equally involved in the communication situation with some overt participatory behavior.

The Explanation Act then is the behavioral environment within which this type of communication takes place. It includes the purpose of the explanation and the subsequent interactions between source and receiver.

The Explanatory Media. The second element in the explanatory model is the media of symbols. Symbolization is seen as the media by which meanings are generated. C. S. Pierce (Buchler: 1955) identifies symbolization as the basic element in all communication. The major contribution of Pierce is his triadic relationship which identifies the three elements of communication as the Sign or Representatem, the Object or Referent, and the Interpretant. Pierces's science of symbols is important to communication because it emphasizes that language represents only concepts or experiences. Words have no meanings in and of themselves;

saves you the trouble of counting characters. The only problem might be with electric typewriters which have variable spacing. They won't line up exactly. You might have to count characters and draw a vertical line with those models of typewriters.

Making the Copy Fit the Space

This approach is used when the design is finished first. In both advertising and magazine design, the layout may be dummied and the copy written to fit.

Writing to fit begins with a layout, a line gauge, a set of type specifications, and an empty typewriter. The procedure is to measure the space to be filled with copy, convert the measure to character counts and lines, and then write to those specifications. The space to be filled may be several pages in a magazine or a small area in an ad or a brochure. With smaller copy areas or copy blocks, the designer will rule in a box or line in a block indicating where the copy goes and how much space it fills.

8. *What is the width in picas of the box?* _____

   What is the depth? _____

First we need to convert the width into the number of characters in a line. Look now to your specifications. They will either be standard for your publication, or will be established by the art director for this job. For our exercise here we will use 10-point Century Schoolbook, with 2 points leading.

9. *Look up the CPP for this face in the table in Appendix 3.* _____

What will the average character count be for a type line that will fit the box?

_____

That character count tells you how to type your copy. You can set your typewriter margins for that length of line.

$$\text{Character Count} = \text{CPP} \times \text{Line Length}$$

In the next calculation, you want to figure how many lines will go in the box. Our designer has given us 10-on-12 Century Schoolbook. Look back at the depth you measured for the box (Exercise 8).

10. *How many lines will fit into that box?*

_____

If you were not using a line height of 12 points, then you would have to first convert the measured height of the box to points and then divide that result by the line height. For example, let's say the designer wanted to use 10-point Century Schoolbook set solid. First you would convert the depth (or height) of the box to points.

$$\text{\# of lines} = \frac{\text{depth} \times 12}{\text{line height}}$$

11. *How many points is the depth of the box?*   _____
    Divide that depth by the line height to get the number of lines which would fit into the box.

_____

You are ready to go. You have obtained the characters-per-line count, set your typewriter for that length of line, and know how many lines you need to type. That's all there is to the problem of writing to fit a given space.

Review Problem. Let's try that procedure over again. Measure the box below and calculate the character count and the number of lines for 8-on-10 News Gothic Bold.

12. *What would be a character count for a line?* _____

    How many lines would you type? _____

Using Typefitting Forms. Here's a tip on writing copy to fit: use a form. You can make one by typing a number guide on the top and bottom of a sheet of paper and then drawing a line down through the characters-per-

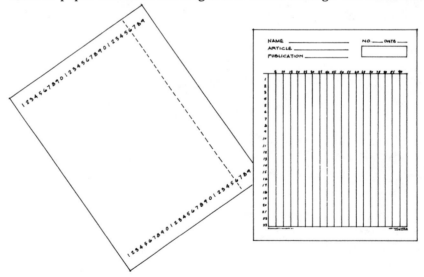

The ABC's of Typography

line number. Some publications have these forms printed with the vertical lines placed for typing at the column widths they regularly use. Others have all their manuscripts typed or retyped on these kinds of forms. Typing to the character counts simplifies their copyfitting, especially if the forms have numbered lines.

Manuscript lines typed on such forms rarely hit the character count exactly, but they should be made to come as close as possible. Being one or two characters under, or four or five over, usually causes no trouble. But if the line length is short (25 characters or fewer), one extra character in the manuscript line may be too many.

Shapes and Run-Arounds. Another use for writing to a character count is to fit the copy around an irregular shape. Though you can give the typesetter a dummy of the shape with instructions to run the copy around it, the type may not fit happily and may require expensive resetting—sometimes once, sometimes more often.

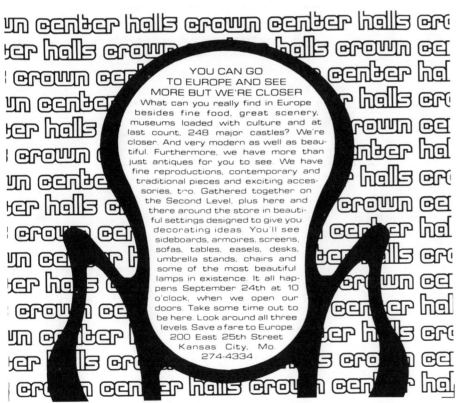

Designed by Dan Proctor & Tina Grant

To be in control of the process, the writer fits the copy line-for-line. Doing this requires calculating the length for each line and writing the copy so it will not produce bad breaks or awkward indentions that would mess up the shape. It is a time-consuming process.

The same kind of process is used for setting copy blocks—in circles or ovals or other shapes. Once again the copy has to be fitted line-for-line.

Let's go through an example step-by-step. You're assigned to write the copy to fit around a cameo illustration. The cameo is your likeness. The copy will describe you. Specifications: 10 on 12 Garamond. Here's the layout:

13. *What is the CPP?*   _____

*What is the line length in the full column above and
   below the cameo?*   _____

*What would be the character count for the full-length
   line?*   _____

What is the length of the shortest lines?   _____

What is the character count for these lines?   _____

The problem now is to figure the progression of the line lengths from the longest to the shortest and then back to the longest. Measure each line.

14. *What is the line-length progression from the full lines to the midpoint and then back to the full lines?*

_____

15. *Convert those measurements to a progression of character counts.*

_____

Write the number of characters for each line down the left side of the accompanying grid.

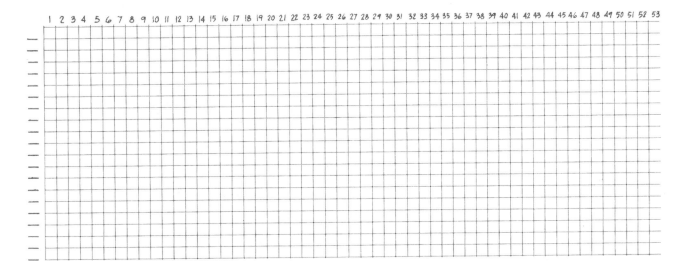

Using one space on the grid for each character, write a description of yourself that fits that character count line by line. Any line may be one character long or short.

Review of Making the Copy Fit the Space

That kind of exercise is a real test of writing skill. Copy written to fit is the editor's headache and the designer's dream. But whether copy must fit space or space must fit copy, the technique of typing on a form simplifies the editing and designing process—especially in writing run-arounds and shaped copy.

16. *For review, write to fit a small copy block. Use the copy here. It is too long, and needs to be edited down to fit the box.*

```
It's easier for Europeans to use Helvetica.  It's very diffcult
for Americans.  We can appeal to big corporate executives with
Helvetica and to stockholders who read annual reports, but for
the great masses of American we cannot do that.  There are over
two thousand typefaces in the world for the masses, and then
there is Helvetica.  Helvetica is for designers, design students,
design instructors, and a few intellectuals and clients, and
for the population of Switzerland.  --Herb Lubalin
```

*Using 10 on 12 Spartan Book, how many characters
    per line?*
How many lines would fit in the box?
Write these lines in the grid below.

Fitting Display Type

Character Count. Few CPP tables give character counts for the type sizes of 24 and 36 points and larger. These sizes are normally display rather than body type and are used for headlines, titles, and subtitles. If you have the CPP for your display type, then you can estimate the length of a headline by multiplying the CPP times the number of characters. (You also can look this up in Appendix 4 rather than multiplying it.)

17. *What's the CPP for 24-point Garamond?* _____

    How long would the following title be in 24-point Garamond?

    _____

```
Manual For Typography
```

Here is the title in the exercise set in that size type. Measure it and see how close your estimate came.

_____

Manual for Typography

Display lines are normally short. If they have fewer than 28 characters, then the width of individual letters may begin to mess up your estimating. For example, "Little Bill Hillbilly" has the same character count as "Manual for Typography."

Little Bill Hillbilly

18. *How many picas does it measure?* _____

Unit Count. On newspapers and periodicals, the columns and typefaces are standardized and the character counts are available in charts and tables. These obviously save time.

But newspapers use another technique to deal with the problem of wide and narrow letters in display type. Headline writers learn early to count by units, not by characters.

Narrow letters like i are each ½ unit. Wide letters like capitals and lower-case m and w are 1½ units. Superwide letters like capital W are two units. Here is the unit counting system:

½ unit: i, l, punctuation, and word space.
1 unit: all other lower-case letters (except m and w); I, and J
1½ unit: m, w, and capital letters except capital M and W
2 unit: capital M and W

Here's how the titles in Exercises 17 and 18 would count:

```
M a n u a l    F o r    T y p o g r a p h y
2 1 1 1 1 1 1 1½ 1 1 1 1½ 1 1 1 1 1 1 1 1 1    = 23
```

```
L i t t l e    B i l l    H i l l b i l l y
1½ ½ 1 1 ½ 1 1  1½ ½ ½ ½ 1  1½ ½ ½ ½ 1 ½ ½ ½ 1    = 17
```

Even though the two titles have the same character count, the first one sets about 36 percent longer. Nor does either title match the line length computed by CPP and character count. The first is longer and the second is shorter. For such reasons, unit-counts are more valuable than character counts for fitting heads.

19. *Count the characters and units in the following heads:*

H o w   t o   M a k e   T h e m   W o r k

_____ units

_____ characters

I t ' s   a   L i t t l e   I n i t i a l

_____ units

_____ characters

Counting units is easy, but editors of newspapers have one other headache. Frequently they are writing to fit extremely tight column widths. A 1-column head in 36-point type may have a count as small as 8 or 9 units.

20. *Write two titles for this book, one for 3 columns in 1 line, and the other for 1 column in 3 lines. Your publication's 1-column head has 10 units and its 3-column head has 32.*

3 columns, 1 line _____

1 column, 3 lines _____

_____

_____

21. *Using the following type specimen, estimate the unit count for 10- and 21-pica lines.*

Newspaper Display Schedule

10 picas: ⎯⎯⎯⎯⎯⎯ units

21 picas: ⎯⎯⎯⎯⎯⎯ units

Schedules. On most publications the unit-count tables, called "headline schedules," are already established. On a new publication, however, someone must prepare a schedule. This is done by taking the publication's typefaces and column widths and counting the units for the pica measure. To do this you would need specimens of your type set in sample headlines. You might be able to use typesetters' specimen books. You also need a line gauge. If your column is 15 picas wide, then measure off 15 picas of the type specimen and count the number of units to that point. To make this estimate more reliable, you might measure and count 15 picas from different segments of the type specimen. If there is any difference in the sample counts, then average them.

22. *Estimate the unit counts for the illustrated sizes of type in a 14-pica column.*

18 The First Duty of Copy Estimators

24 The First Duty of Copy Esti

36 The First Duty of

48 The First Du

The ABC's of Typography

18 point: ─────────────

24 point: ─────────────

36 point: ─────────────

48 point: ─────────────

The unit-count system is very useful for standardized column widths and a limited number of typefaces. When a wide variety of display type is available and line length varies, another method of estimating is needed.

Display Comparison. Display comparison is a method discussed by Edmund Arnold for quickly checking the fit of a line of display. You will need a type specimen book from your typesetter and your line gauge.

Most specimen books have a phrase which they set in the various typefaces and sizes. Write or type that phrase on a piece of paper. Then type your display copy letter-by-letter underneath that phrase. In order to make this estimate more reliable, you might leave extra spaces for the letters that make 1½ or 2 units.

```
The first duty of copy estimators is to...

A M anual of Typography
```

The title here ends before the letter E in the phrase from the type specimen book. If you know you want to set the title in 36-point, then turn to the specimen book and measure the 36-point line to the space before this E. That measure tells you how long your title will be in 36-point.

23. *Using these specimens for 24- and 36-point type, measure how long the title "The Language of Printers" would set in picas.*

The First Duty of Copy Estimators

24 point: _____

The First Duty of Copy Esti

36 point: _____

If, on the other hand, you need to make that line fit into a specified column width, then measure down the lines of type specimens until you find the largest one that measures out to that width or less at the end of the letter E. For example, if you were using an 18-pica column width, you would use the 24-point type in the series of Exercises 22 and 23 for the title, *A Manual of Typography.*

24. *If you wanted to fit the title "Amazing Copyfitter" into a 26-pica line, which size in the Copperplate Gothic specimens on the next page would you use?*

_____

The ABC's of Typography

10 COPPERPLATE GOTHIC HEAVY

12 COPPERPLATE GOTHIC HEAVY

18 COPPERPLATE GOTHIC

24 COPPERPLATE GO

Review of Estimating Display Type

Now you have three ways to estimate type for display.

The character-count method is good primarily for long lines of type in smaller sizes.

The unit-count method works well for display lines in periodicals or for other kinds of typesetting which involve standardized faces and line lengths.

The comparison method works best for estimating display where there is a variety of faces and sizes—as in advertising or brochure design. Another way to estimate display type by comparison is to trace the letters from your specimen book. If you have a complete alphabet available, then this is probably the most reliable of all methods.

Estimates made by these methods are not invariably correct but they are all more reliable than no method at all. It is cheaper to make copy fit when it is in the typewriter than after the type has been set.

Chapter 7

Type Specifying

As an editor or designer, you are expected to give clear and complete instructions to the typesetter. Like an architect working on blueprints, you have to anticipate and answer every question your printer (like the builder) might have. Unless you answer the questions ahead of time, your printer will devise answers. Nine times out of ten, those answers are not the same ones you would have given.

These instructions to typesetters and printers are written in a technical language that they share with editors and designers. It includes code and shorthand that have to be learned. Until it is learned, its symbols may look like meaningless hieroglyphics. (A set of editor's marks is given in Appendix 5, pages 180–183).

Body Copy

In specifying body copy there are four essential pieces of information: the typeface, the size, the line length, and the amount of leading. Line length is expressed in picas, type size and leading in points (until metric measurements come into use). When placed on the manuscript, this information is part of the "mark-up." (See example on next page.)

To specify the amount of leading you will say something like "10 on 12" or "9 on 10." This kind of expression comes from the hot-metal days when a 10-point type was actually cast on a metal slug that was 12 points from top to bottom. That puts two points space between the lines. If no leading was wanted, you might say "10 on 10" or "10 solid." This piece of information contains both the type size and the amount of space between the lines, which together gives you the line height.

Considering the simple appearance of a sans serif, sober and bare as it is, one would think of it as a pretty rigid construction rather than fashioned with any sensibility. Yet, in a sans serif face, the shapes of letters should be related to a free-hand drawing; curves never drawn with compasses, straight lines not always straight and hardly ever parallel. Serifs should be looked upon somewhat as bridges between signs, the lack of suitable links being made up for by a tighter fit in just the right proportion, so that white spaces inside letters correctly match the white spaces between letters. --Adrian Frutiger

1. *How would you write the specifications for 12-point type with no space between lines? How for 12-point type with a space between the lines that is equal to one-third of the type size?*

The ABC's of Typography

These three elements—the size, the line length or column width, and the leading—are usually written together as a formula. The form of the formula will vary from printer to printer, but three of the most common forms are shown here:

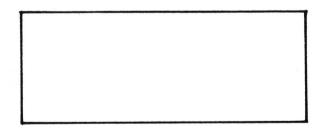

a. 13/10 on 12 Helvetica

b. 10/12 Helvetica × 13

c. 10/12 Helvetica
        13

2. *Write the mark-up for the copy block which will fit in the space shown. To start specify 10-point Century.*

Column Edges

There are four common ways your lines can be set in columns: justified, ragged right, ragged left, and centered. This is another instruction that your typesetter needs to know.

Flush left,
ragged right

A graphic designer is not only indebted to Baroque, but cannot ignore what has been and is being created in such diverse fields as architecture, sculpture, literature, music, theater, and dance.

—Massin

Flush right
ragged left

A graphic designer is not only indebted to Baroque, but cannot ignore what has been and is being created in such diverse fields as architecture, sculpture, literature, music, theater, and dance.

Centered
or
ragged right
and left

A graphic designer is not only indebted to Baroque, but cannot ignore what has been and is being created in such diverse fields as architecture, sculpture, literature music, theater, and dance.

Justified
or
flush right
and left

A graphic designer is not only indebted to Baroque, but cannot ignore what has been and is being created in such diverse fields as architecture, sculpture, literature music, theater, and dance.

The ABC's of Typography

Justified Columns. When copy is set "justified," the margins are straight on both sides; the lines are full. The amount of space between the words will vary from line to line to make the lines equal. For the spaces between the words to look equal your lines usually need at least 50 characters. Shorter lines will often appear to have "holes" where they need wide word spacing to make the even column edge.

Centered Columns. The opposite of justified copy is centered copy. All the spacing between words is equal and no lines align on either column edge. This kind of copy is used most frequently for formal invitations. One word of caution: this style of typesetting should be used only for small amounts of copy because the lack of any hard edge makes it difficult to read more than a few lines without getting lost.

To specify centered copy you mark it in two ways. First you write "centered" below your mark-up formula. Second you use printer's marks to indicate precisely what copy is to be centered. These marks are illustrated.

11 on 12 Garamond
12 centered

Today's type designer has to be highly

skilled, a combination of engineer and

artist, with patience to master the

technical intricacies, but with the

independence to remain as intent as

ever upon serving the artistic needs of

man as well as the mechanical needs of

the devices. --John Dreyfus

Ragged Columns. Sometimes you will see copy set unjustified on one side, either the right or left. There are two different ways to describe this. You can say "flush left" or "flush right," which means the column edge is even or "flush" on the indicated side, you can say "ragged right" or "ragged left," which means the opposite. A column that is ragged right will probably be flush left. A column that is ragged left will probably be flush right. Printers tend to use the form which refers to the right column edge. Someone may occasionally say "flush left," but most instructions are either "flush right" or "ragged right."

Your specifications for ragged settings also need both the formula and the symbols marked on the copy. The mark up will look like this:

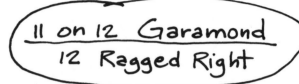

One of the most exacting areas of design is to update the past in terms of the present.   --Matthew Carter

Since most copy is set justified, you don't have to indicate that specification. Only when you want centered or ragged setting do you have to give instructions for the column edge. Your typesetter may also want to know how ragged the edge should be. This will usually be 2 or 3 ems but may vary with the width of the line. Also, you will need to decide whether or not to use hyphenation.

3. *Mark up the next piece of copy for setting on 12-point Baskerville with 2 points of space between lines which are to be 15 picas long. The copy will be set ragged right except for the quotation, which is to be set centered.*

Graphic design deals with space. It is inherent in man to

seek order in space. Like a picture hanging crooked on the

wall, isolated and unrelated elements cry for readjustment.

How does typography relate to design? One definition is:

    "Typography is to printing

      as dramatics and elocution

      are to the spoken word."

Run-Arounds. Another type of variation in column edge comes from "run arounds," which are copy blocks of unusual shapes. There are several ways to specify runaround composition. One of the surest is to give the compositor the length for each line along with a layout and line-for-line manuscript that has been character-counted to fit the line lengths. The compositor will set justified lines to these lengths. This method was explained in Chapter 6. It is easier if the copy can be written or edited to fit. If the compositor gets copy without all these guides, he must figure the line lengths. At the least, it is a good idea to furnish an exact outline of the art and a drawing of the copy block along with the copy.

On the following page is sample copy which has been typed for a runaround. After it appears copy which has been set line for line and another sample which has been set justified to fit a shape.

Original typed copy:

The future hope of printing lies in
the new miracles of film and
electronic setting by
which the whole art
will be revolution-
ized, for good or
for bad. If these
new techniques only
replace craftsmen by
inhuman mechanism,
they will fail. They
will succeed if, by immeas-
urably increasing his resources,
they reinstate the conscious and
unconscious powers of the human
artist. --Alvin Eisenman

Copy set line for line:

The future hope of printing lies in
the new miracles of film and
electronic setting by
which the whole art
will be revolution-
ized, for good or
for bad. If these
new techniques only
replace craftsmen by
inhuman mechanism,
they will fail. They
will succeed if, by immeas-
urably increasing his resources,
they reinstate the conscious and
unconscious powers of the human
artist. —Alvin Eisenman

Copy set justified to a shape:

> The future hope of printing lies in
> the new miracles of film and
> electronic setting by
> which the whole art
> will be revolution-
> ized, for good or
> for bad. If these
> new techniques only
> replace craftsmen by
> inhuman mechanism,
> they will fail. They
> will succeed if, by immeas-
> urably increasing his resources,
> they reinstate the conscious and
> unconscious powers of the human
> artist.   —Alvin Eisenman

Indentions. A typesetter will normally indent a paragraph one em. If you do not want any indention, specify that the first line should be flush left. If you want more indention than normal, you must specify it. This is particularly true if you want space for an oversize initial letter or some other ornament. You also must specify size in ems for "hang indentions" where the body copy is indented under the first line. The following indention mark-up is shown in typeset copy on the next page:

indent
1

> Much modern typography
>
> startles, identifies, charms,
>
> and even illustrates. Designers
>
> prime little typographic
>
> explosions to go off with a
>
> flash and a visual noise at
>
> the turning of a page.
>
>   --Aaron Burns

Much modern typography
startles, identifies, charms,
and even illustrates. De-
signers prime little typographic explosions to go off
with a flash and a visual noise
at the turning of a page.
—Aaron Burns

4. *The following copy is to be set 10 on 12 Futura. The paragraph will begin with an initial letter which is 3 picas square. Specify the indention.*

Calligraphy properly defined is writing or

lettering of pleasing excellence. What is

excellence? I answer this question

obliquely by pointing to the pragmatic

fact that Imperial majuscules have been

accepted in practically each age since

the Imperium as the pinnacle of calligraphic

achievement in the Western world.

--Edward M. Catich

Spacing

Additional line spacing is sometimes needed between paragraphs, above illustrations and tables, and around subtitles. If you don't specify any, you may get a crowded horror from your typesetter. If you want any extra spacing anywhere in the copy, you have to tell your typesetter how much and where. The crowded material would look different and better if the manuscript had been marked to specify the proper spacing.

Copyfitting

The Perfect Balance

Copyfitting is the process of trying to figure out before you send your copy to the printer, how much copy you have and how much space it will fill.

1. Estimating Copy and Fitting Space. This is the writer's favorite method. The words are on paper first and the designer has to make the space fit them.

2. Estimating Space and Fitting Copy. This is the designer's favorite method because the writer has to do the fitting and make the words fit the space.

The secret to copyfitting is this: Establish one of the variables and fit the other.

Copyfitting

The Perfect Balance

Copyfitting is the process of trying to figure out before you send your copy to the printer, how much copy you have and how much space it will fill.

1. Estimating Copy and Fitting Space. This is the writer's favorite method. The words are on paper first and the designer has to make the space fit them.

2. Estimating Space and Fitting Copy. This is the designer's favorite method because the writer has to do the fitting and make the words fit the space.

The secret to copyfitting is this: Establish one of the variables and fit the other.

Spacing is measured in points, the same as leading, and the symbol #
is used in writing the spacing instructions. Examine the manuscript as it
would be marked to get the material set in the improved version

Copyfitting
⟨+4 pts #⟩

The Perfect Balance
⟨+2 pts #⟩

Copyfitting is the process of trying to figure out

before you send your copy to the printer, how much

copy you have and how much space it will fill.
⟨+2 pts #⟩

1. Estimating Copy and Fitting Space. This is the

writer's favorite method. The words are on paper

first and the designer has to make the space fit them.
⟨+2 pts #⟩

2. Estimating Space and Fitting Copy. This is the

designer's favorite method because the writer has

to do the fitting and make the words fit the space.
⟨+2 pts #⟩

The secret to copyfitting is this: Establish one

of the variables and fit the other.

5. *Mark the spacing in the outline on the following page. Specify twice as
much spacing before Roman-numeral lines as before letter lines and
twice as much before letter lines as before the descriptive paragraphs.
Begin with 8 points spacing before the Roman-numeral lines.*

The ABC's of Typography

I. Estimating Copy--Fitting the Space

    A. What are the type specifications?

       Find or figure the cpp. Establish the line width.

       Figure the average character count by line.

    B. How much copy is in the manuscript?

       Estimate the average character count and count

       the lines

    C. How many lines will the manuscript equal in typeset

       copy?

       Since you know the manuscript character count and number

       of lines as well as the typeset character count, you

       can find the number of lines on a proportion wheel.

II. Estimating Space--Fitting the Copy

    A. What's the character count for your line?

       Calculate the typeset character count from the

       specifications. Set your typewriter at that count.

    B. How many lines long?

       Measure the space in picas and convert to points.

       Divide by the line height for the total number of lines.

    C. How do you write to fit?

       Set your typewriter at the character count and type the

       number of lines you calculated.

Style Marks

Another part of specifying is to mark up the manuscript to indicate where variations within the type family are to be used. There are three common variations: boldface, italics, and capitals. Boldface and capitals are used to convey emphasis. Italics are used to indicate that something is different or separate from the body copy. Italics do not necessarily convey emphasis. Because they have lighter strokes they may even suggest lesser importance. Some designers feel that italics are best used to indicate something different, such as introductory statements or photo captions, rather than emphasis.

Boldface is indicated with a wavy underscore. Italic is indicated with a straight underscore. Capitals are indicated by three-line underscore. It's wise to mark up the copy with both symbols and words, particularly since not all printers use the same symbols for boldface and italics.

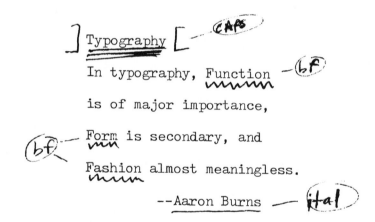

Compare the same copy in marked-up manuscript and in type on the following page:

] Design and Cost [*Bfc*

The Cost of Quality *Pica #*   *ital*
— *6 pts #*

Although it is seldom achieved, perfection is used

as a yardstick for evaluating accomplishments. In all

phases of typography, and particularly advertising

typography, perfection would probably be most nearly

achieved with an adequate supply of new type and no

concern for the cost of compostion. However, most of

the jobs produced for advertising do not allow either

money or time to attain perfection.

DESIGN AND COST

The Cost of Quality

Although it is seldom achieved, *perfection* is
used as a yardstick for evaluating accomplishments. In all phases of typography, and
particularly advertising typography, *perfection* would probably be most nearly achieved
with an adequate supply of new type and no
concern for the cost of composition. However, most of the jobs produced for advertising do not allow either money or time to
attain *perfection.*

6. *Mark up the manuscript (Notes about Folks) to specify boldface capitals for headings, boldface for names, and italics for cities.*

Notes About Folks

Karen J. Beck, Shawnee Mission, an elementary teacher was selected as an Outstanding Elementary Teacher of America.

Dr. Alvin L. Lewis, Anderson, has accepted the position of associate secretary of the Board of Christian Education.

Robert D. Wehling, Oil City, is assistant to the director of fiscal services in hospital fiscal management.

Deaths

Jessie A. Arnold, Jacksonville, on October 6.

Charles F. Croyle, Hutchinson, on January 15. He is survived by his widow, five children and 23 grandchildren.

Births

Susan (Miller) and Calvin Schwartz, Pawnee Peak, a daughter, Jane Elizabeth, on July 25.

Display Copy

Display-copy manuscript is much easier than body copy to specify and mark up. Compositors like to separate display from body manuscript since the two are usually set on different machines. (Some machines can set both display and body type at the same time; check with your printer.) The display copy should be typed on separate pages and marked to show its place in the body copy.

Examine a sample lot of display-type manuscript marked up for composition.

60 Souvenir Bold — The Spirited Marching Machine

60 Souvenir — Athletics Pinched by Financial Squeeze

48 Souvenir Ital. — A Season to Remember

48 Souvenir — Family Camp is an Education Vacation

36 Souvenir Ital. — President Steals the Show

36 Souvenir Bold — Concern over Salary Sparks Meeting

36 Souvenir — Football Kick-offs Begin With Pre-Game Buffet *(lc.)*

24 Souvenir — Creative Arts Board Recommends Historical Listing

18 Souvenir Bold — A Clock with Four Faces

18 Souvenir Ital. — Hoopla Runs in Circles

There are two basic things to specify for display: typeface and size. You may also specify column width for publications with standardized formats. Generally the display for ads and job work is set flush. Hence it is rarely necessary to give the typesetter column-edge instructions.

In addition, you may need to specify letter spacing. This is commonly indicated with a caret between the feet of the two letters to be spaced. With computer typesetting, which has the capability for minus spacing (tight setting) you may specify plus or minus one, two, or three units. These numbers are marked under the caret sign. The vertical letters, i and l, may be plus spaced up to two units. The round letters such as o, c, d, b, a, and e can be left normal or closed up one unit. Minus spacing is most often used with kerned letters. If both letters kern, as do AY, then you can decrease the space between them as much as two units. If only one letter kerns, as in AM, you probably should try minus spacing one unit. Three units of plus or minus spacing is appropriate only for deliberately distorted effects—which usually decreases readability.

L∧e∧t∧e r s
-1 -1 +1 -1

l∧i∧t∧l e   m∧o∧r∧e
+1 +1 +1 +1   -1 -1 -1

Y∧A∧W∧L
-2 -2 -1

Before you try letterspacing mark-up, check with your typesetter to make sure the equipment has the capability to do letterspacing. The size of units will vary from machine to machine, ask for a sample of various units of letterspacing before you specify your type. Your typesetter may prefer that you not specify units but use words like *close*, *tight* and *touching*.

The ABC's of Typography

7. *Mark this all-caps headline where you would decrease and increase letter spacing.*

M I N I T O W N   L O O K S   L I K E   S P A C E   T O Y

Review of Specifications

Display type is the easiest to specify; only face and size need to be indicated. Body type is more complicated. The four things to be specified are:

Typeface	Leading
Type size	Line length or column width

Other special instructions for body type may include:

Column edges:	Line spacing
Ragged right	Style marks
Flush right	Boldface
Centered	Italic
Runarounds	Capitals
Indentions	

8. *In this set of specifications for body copy, what is missing?*

_____

9. *Mark the paragraph on the following page for flush-right setting.*

Edmund Arnold says, "We 'read' words and phrases by recognizing their silhouettes, especially their top one. The silhouette of a word in lowercase or upper-and-lower is distinctive."

10. *In this copy, mark the magazine title to be set boldface and the quotation to be set in italics.*

Harper's Bazaar dominated design. Its art director, Alexey Brodovitch, "kept apprentices at his side much like an Old World master painter."

Proofreader Marks

The language used by designers, editors, and typesetters includes signs, symbols, and abbreviations used on manuscripts and on proofs to indicate changes and corrections.

Two different systems of marks are used. Manuscript copy is typed double spaced and contains the copy-editing marks within the body of the copy. In proof, only location marks are placed in the copy; instruction marks go in the margin.

Similar or identical marks are used for copyediting and proofreading. Some of them, such as space and style marks, are already familiar to you. A complete set of marks and signs is included in Appendix 5 (page 180).

Copyediting is the correcting and marking process done on the manuscript by the editor. Words, spelling, grammar, and style are checked. Every questionable fact is verified. The editor's challenge is to catch all possible errors at this point—before the type is set.

After the manuscript is typeset a proof is pulled. This is proofread—checked for typographical errors—by both the typesetter and the editor.

The ABC's of Typography

The editor also checks to see that the specifications were followed—type size, face, column width, leading, and special instructions. If the original manuscript was copyedited by a conscientious editor, then the only changes at this stage will be corrections for typographical mistakes.

Corrections made on manuscript:

Optima, designed and manufactured
on the New Word is classyc in
design. It brings up to date a
Roman alphabet which preYates
the Christian era. Many attempts
have been made to produce a face
based on these early Roman
letter fYdms, but non except
Optima has captured the subtile
grace and balance.

Same corrections made on galley proof:

Optima, designed and manufactured øn the
New Word is classyc in design. It brings up
to date a Roman alphabet which preyates the
Christian era. Many attempts have been
made to produce a face based on these early
Roman letter frdms, but non except Optima
has captured the subtile grace and balance.

/i
/l /i
/d

/tr /e
/s

11. *Read the following proof against the manuscript and make all necessary corrections.*

Original manuscript:

The Univers family of faces is a contemporary all-purpose, sans serif. The entire series of faces in all its variations has been worked out in detail from a simple basic design to form a single integrated family. Univers should end the compromises which designers have had to make repeatedly because of the lack of type face concept and designs to fit their needs. Univers is a completely new concept in type design which brings the total integration of all the elements in the design of a type face in all sizes, widths, and bodies. Univers is a complete family designed as a family.

Galley proof:

The Univers family of races is a contemporary all-purpose, sens serif. The entire series of faces in all its variations has been worked out in detale from a simple basic design to form a simple integrated family. Universe should end the compromises which designers have make repetedly because of the lack of type face concept and designs to fit their needs. Univers is a completely new concept in type design which brings the total integration of all the elements in the design of a elements in the design of a type face in all sizes, widths, and bodies. Univers is a complate family designed as a family.

The ABC's of Typography

Editorial changes made in proof can really chew up the budget. Type-setters do not (or should not) charge for correcting their errors, but they do charge for resetting to correct editors' errors—"author's alterations." There is no ceiling on such charges. The reason they are so costly is that one small change may involve resetting a large amount of type. If you insert one word, perhaps even one letter, into justified copy, then the entire paragraph from that line on may have to be reset in order to make room for it. In the following paragraph notice how a change in the second line affects the justification for the rest of the paragraph:

First Proof:

To develop a system of classification for designs we must be able to see the difference between the basic geometric shapes that provide mere letter recognition, and the creative designing that elaborates these shapes—that gives them individuality and enables them to be classified.
                                                    —Edward Rondthaler

Revised Proof:

To develop a system of classification for typeface designs we must be able to see the differences between the basic geometric shapes that provide mere letter recognition, and the creative designing that elaborates these shapes—that gives them individuality and enables them to be classified.
                                                    —Edward Rondthaler

Proofreading is a two-operation process. The editor should check the specifications and read through the proof for meaning. The proofreading for typographical errors is best done by two people. One reads the manuscript and the other follows the typeset copy. This voice-and-scan process is the only reliable way to proofread for typos. One person can, of course, read the proof alone. Such a single reader may easily miss a departure from the manuscript. Those who jump back and forth between manuscript and the proof are subject to a second hazard, the proofreader's syndrome. Psychologists have commented on this from a perceptual standpoint: you see only what you expect to see. Particularly if you saw the copy before it was typeset—if you are either the writer or the editor—you may find yourself reading what you think will be there, rather than what is actually on the page.

When proofreading is done by two people, the one who marks the proof should be totally unfamiliar with the manuscript. If you have to proofread your own manuscript, then read the proof first and look back at the manuscript to check for omissions or repeats and to verify numbers and the spellings of names.

After the proof has been returned to the typesetter, a revised proof with corrections should be requested, particularly if there were a lot of changes. Also, an old printers' joke insists that you always make more errors when correcting errors. In particular, watch for corrections that have been inserted into the wrong place.

12. *Mark up this manuscript. First read it through for typing errors. Then mark it to be set in 8-point Garamond with 2 points leading. The column width will be 13 picas. Leave an indention at the beginning of the first paragraph for a symbol which is 2 picas wide and 2 picas deep. All typeface titles should be in italic and persons' names in bold-face. Have the paragraph set ragged right.*

Clarendon

The original Clarendon is a Roman type face which
has been used for many years by technical book
publishers when a boldfact is desirable to
differentiat scientific names from the text. Its
usefullness stems from the extra wieght of the serife
and its blackness compared with normal Roman. The
American designer, Freeman Craw, has extended this
usefulness by creating there distinct weights of
Clarendon for American Type Founders.

Chapter 8

Readability and Legibility

Legibility is the functional aspect of typography. If you are concerned with legibility, you ask: How well does it read? How easily can the reader perceive the meaning behind these printed letter forms?

Typographers have operated on the theory that the eye is an impatient observer and the slightest annoyance may force it from the page. Recent psychological research in the reading process tends to support this view.

The action of reading is a highly rhythmic scanning process. The eye stops at regular intervals and fixes on a group of letter forms as a single unit. These are called saccadic eye movements and there are several in a long line. Sometimes the scan stops and regresses to read a unit over again. The stop-and-regress action contributes to eye fatigue.

When a reader is deeply engrossed in a subject, like when you read a good novel or a physicist reads the report of a new breakthrough, the mechanics of reading become relatively unimportant. You could print occasional letters upside down and the deeply engrossed reader would continue to read.

Readers who are only minimally engrossed or not interested at all, like the physics student on the night of a big game, will find their eyes and mind bouncing off the page at the slightest interruption. For these readers, as well as those who scan the headlines and ads in thousands of newspapers, magazines, and television screens, we must use the forms of type easiest to read.

Two factors are involved in ease of reading: readability and legibility. Readability describes the understanding of the message. Legibility describes the process of discriminating and recognizing individual letter forms.

Generally, we use the term readability when referring to such things as word choice and sentence length. Legibility more usually applies to size, type and shape of the letter forms.

Guidelines have been developed for questions relating to both legibility and readability. Some are based on scientific research, some on the experienced observations of typographers, editors, and designers. Few of them are rules that can't be broken. Many are open to interpretation, even to contradiction. But they are available to help editors and designers who are concerned about attracting and keeping the reader's eye.

Legibility

Type Design. There seems to be agreement among the experienced observers as well as the academic researchers that sans serif display type is easier to see than the roman types. The larger the letter, the simpler its design needs to be.

Have you ever seen a stop sign in roman letters with delicate serifs? Observe the signs around you: the building signs, street signs, and billboards. They are dominated by sans serif letters.

The ABC's of Typography

In some instances display type offers unanticipated information and has to be read—like the headline on a billboard—but in many cases, the type forms a pattern that comes to be anticipated and recognized by its distinctive shape, which then serves to attract the eye.

This is the label effect of display type, and it works best after repeated exposures. The designer's goal is to create a graphic image that is distinctive, attractive, and immediately recognizable. Distortion may serve this goal. Readability becomes less important than recognizability.

Designed by Murray Smith and Michael Doret

In some cases, however, the sign makers are more concerned with readability than with labeling. We see this particularly along the highway, where advertisers and highway engineers are trying to get information to a reader whizzing by at 55 miles an hour. Display which needs to be read easily is more effective in common, familiar, easy-to-process letter shapes than in distinctive and unusual patterns.

In general, ornamented faces are harder to see than simple letter styles. While a fancy design may contribute something distinctive, it sacrifices legibility. You very seldom see large display in black letters, cursive, or italic forms.

1. *If you had a choice between Garamond and Helvetica for parking-lot signs, which would you choose?*

A face can be too simple, however. Also, the highly geometrical faces which distort the distinctive shapes of the letters are difficult to read. You have probably experienced that difficulty with the machine-readable type on your checks and utility bills.

2. *If you are designing the logo to go with a "country store" image, will you use Caslon or Helvetica?*

3. *Of the four typeface alphabets, which one would you pick for setting the display copy in an advertisement for a bank?*

1   abcdefghijklmnopqrstuvwxyz

2   ABCDEFGHIJKLMNOPQRSTUVWXYZ

3   abbbbbbbccddddeeefgggghhijkklmm

4   abcdefghijklmnopqrstuvwxyz

All Caps. Type that is set in all-capitals is harder to read than type in upper and lowercase letters. All-cap lines are like the geometrical faces—they have smooth edges. The irregularities of the lower-case coastlines serve the eye as signposts for recognizing words and letters. Observe the four type samples in all-caps.

READABILITY IS THE CHALLENGE
READABILITY IS THE CI
READABILITY IS THE CHALL
READABILITY IS THE CHAL

The ABC's of Typography

The outline shape of the word is what is perceived by the eye. The scanning process focuses on the top half of the word and the right sides of the letters.

4. *Glance quickly at the two cut-off lines. Which is the phrase you identified first?*

ui uupy Lsiimaiuis

Tho First Dutv

That wasn't a very scientific experiment, but it should demonstrate to you the way your eye has become trained to recognize letter forms by their upper coastlines.

When you use all-caps, you eliminate the very important upper coastline and that slows down reading. Compare two samples of the same typeface and check yourself. Which do you think is easiest to read?

Oracle Bold   **ORACLE BOLD**

Probably the only "thou shalt not" in the typography business applies to all-caps. Avoid using all-caps in italic, cursive, or black letters. See for yourself. How quickly can you decipher the three lines:

GARAMOND ITALIC CAPS

MURRAY HILL CAPS

CAXTON INITIALS

You might as well have been looking at a sign language or a secret code. Capitals are difficult enough to read; when they are combined with unusual or highly ornamented letter forms, they are virtually unreadable.

Close Setting and Wide Spacing. There is little agreement about close setting. Ligatures and kerns have been used since the beginning of printing to eliminate awkward space between letters that are frequently used together. As these devices are commonly used, they can speed up the scanning process and are a definite asset to reading and type texture.

To achieve close setting, a number of modern faces have been designed with unusual ligatures. But many editors and designers consider these faces difficult to read. The question is whether such ligatures increase the speed of reading as they become more familiar or stop the process entirely because they are unusual. What do you think?

Until these ligatures become commonplace, they probably will slow down the unprepared reader. But since reading speed ultimately is on their side, I would predict that these ligatures will continue to gain acceptability and eventually become common in the printer's alphabets.

Ligatures are the ultimate in close setting, but when we speak of close setting we usually refer to the space between independent letters. The use of negative spacing and kerning is common with display type. It pulls large letters into groups which are easier to scan. Compare wide-set and close-set samples.

The ABC's of Typography

The secret of effective close setting is to eliminate only that space between letters which is unnecessary to recognition. For example, a and e can be set close and still be recognized. If you close set i and l touching, then the letters will no longer be legible.

Researchers have found what is important is the proportion of the space between letters to the size of the letters and the distance between the words. Close-set type, unless it is extreme, does not seem to hinder the recognition of display type. Wide letter spacing, on the other hand, can break up a word and cause a legibility problem.

The goal of optical spacing in display type is to even out the density. Typographers have felt that the uneven contrast of light and dark masses is a hindrance to legibility, that the concentration of dark forces the eye to pause and break its scanning pattern. While this feeling has not been demonstrated scientifically, aesthetics would certainly suggest that a limited use of letter spacing—both tight and wide—would be wise.

Many of the findings and theories relating to display also apply to body copy. Highly ornamented faces and all-capitals are difficult to read. Spacing should be proportional—too much between letters makes the words fall apart and too much between words creates awkward vertical rivers of white in a copy block. Close-set copy however, may present more of a legibility problem.

Type Design. The main difference between the legibility of display type and of body copy is demonstrated by the sans serif. This is a major area of controversy in typography. Sans serif faces are recognized as easier to see, but not necessarily easier to read.

A number of experts are wary of using sans serif for large amounts of copy. Edmund Arnold is probably the spokesman for this viewpoint. Arnold feels that the serifs on the roman faces serve a definite function in the rhythmic reading pattern. The serifs are distinctive features of each letter which help aid recognition; they are also little connectors which tie the letters together in groups.

A research study conducted recently by Hvistendahl and Kahl found that the reading speed of newspaper readers was significantly lower with sans serif than with roman faces.

Critics of roman letters say that the serifs serve no useful purpose in the perception of type and the only reason readers seem to prefer type with serifs is that they learned to read from books printed with serif faces.

5. *Compare two columns of type set in roman and sans serif. Read them both and see if you can tell or feel any difference in the speed of your reading. They are both set 10 on 12.*

1. Newly invented letters, however ingenious, are not likely to become widely accepted. . . . The demand that we make of a typeface is not simplicity, but legibility along with familiar letterforms, must be preserved in the future, despite technical developments that may still arise.—Max Caflisch

2. Newly invented letters, however ingenious, are not likely to become widely accepted. . . . The demand that we make of a typeface is not simplicity, but legibility along with familiar letterforms, must be preserved in the future, despite technical developments that may still arise.—Max Caflisch

Which face do you prefer?

_____

Type size. A number of studies have been conducted to determine what size of body type has the best legibility. The recommended sizes are from 9- to 12-point, according to Rolf Rehe, who has surveyed a number of studies relating to legibility.

8 on 10
Helvetica

Complex problems in the sphere of verbal-visual communication cannot be solved by one person alone. They demand the cooperation of many people (e.g. publicity consultants, copy writers, sociologists, compositors, printers) and also the client, as a great deal of fundamental information is only obtainable from him. The typographer and his work is therefore only a part of the whole.
—Ruedi Ruegg and Godi Fohlich

10 on 12
Helvetica

Complex problems in the sphere of verbal-visual communication cannot be solved by one person alone. They demand the cooperation of many people (e.g. publicity consultants, copy writers, sociologists, compositors, printers) and also the client, as a great deal of fundamental information is only obtainable from him. The typographer and his work is therefore only a part of the whole.
—Ruedi Ruegg and Godi Fohlich

12 on 14
Helvetica

Complex problems in the sphere of verbal-visual communication cannot be solved by one person alone. They demand the cooperation of many people (e.g. publicity consultants, copy writers, sociologists, compositors, printers) and also the client, as a great deal of fundamental information is only obtainble from him. The typographer and his work is therefore only a part of the whole.
—Ruedi Ruegg and Godi Fohlich

Line Length. Optimum line length is closely related to the question of type size. The bigger the type, the longer the line should be. The smaller the type, the shorter the line length. Given the optimum type sizes of 9- to 12-

12 on 14 Helvetica
13 picas

Complex problems in the sphere of verbal-visual communication cannot be solved by one person alone. They demand the cooperation of many people (e.g. publicity consultants, copy writers, sociologists, compositors, printers) and also the client, as a great deal of fundamental information is only obtainable from him. The typographer and his work is therefore only a part of the whole.
—Ruedi Ruegg and Godi Fohlich

10 on 12
Helvetica
20 picas

Complex problems in the sphere of verbal-visual communication cannot be solved by one person alone. They demand the cooperation of many people (e.g. publicity consultants, copy writers, sociologists, compositors, printers) and also the client, as a great deal of fundamental information is only obtainable from him. The typographer and his work is therefore only a part of the whole.
—Ruedi Ruegg and Godi Fohlich

8 on 10
Helvetica
26 picas

Complex problems in the sphere of verbal-visual communication cannot be solved by one person alone. They demand the cooperation of many people (e.g. publicity consultants, copy writers, sociologists, compositors, printers) and also the client, as a great deal of fundamental information is only obtainable from him. The typographer and his work is therefore only a part of the whole.

—Ruedi Ruegg and Godi Fohlich

point, the recommended line length would be from 18 to 24 picas, according to Rehe. Of the sample paragraphs on the preceeding page, the line length is too short for the type size in the first paragraph. In the last, the line length is too long for the type size. The middle paragraph is a better balance of type size and line length.

There are two other ways to choose optimum line length. Printers have said that the best length is 1½ times the length of a lower-case alphabet. Since most printers provide a specimen book with alphabets printed, you can simply measure that length in your choosen type size and then multiply the length by 1½.

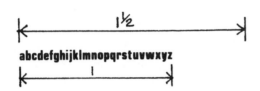

Another way to calculate line length is based on point size and gives a maximum length rather than an optimum. The rule is: Use a line length no longer than twice the point size of the type. For using 8-point type, then, the line should not be over 16 picas long; for 10-point type, not over 20 picas.

Both of these methods provide guidelines which have been generally substantiated by research.

Leading. A factor related to both type size and line length is leading. The space between the lines performs a necessary function. It separates the upper coastline of a line from the bottom coastline of the preceding line, thereby providing an alley of white which guides the eye back to the beginning of the next line. If that alley is not in proportion to the size of the type and the length of the line, then the eye may not start to resume its scanning on the right line.

Research indicates that the optimum type sizes (9 to 12 point) in an optimum line length (18 to 24 picas) should have from 1 point to 2 points of leading between the lines.

Column Edges. The effect of justified lines on legibility is another area of disagreement. Traditionally typographers and editors have felt that justified lines are easier to read. Edmund Arnold explains that the "hard edge" on the right side of the column gives the eye something to bounce off in its rhythmic back-and-forth scan pattern.

Recent research does not indicate that justified lines are any easier to read than unjustified lines. Contemporary designers argue that ragged-right copy is more natural in that words don't have to be hyphenated. Experience has determined, in any case, that unjustified copy is easier and cheaper to produce.

> Typography is a means to an end and not an end in itself, and it is, therefore, an activity which is necessarily subject to certain restraints.
> —Herbert Spencer

> Typography is a means to an end and not an end in itself, and it is, therefore, an activity which is necessarily subject to certain restraints.
> —Herbert Spencer

Most designers and editors agree that ragged-left and centered copy is difficult to read. A definite beginning edge seems to be necessary for readers who read from left to right. On the following page compare the paragraph set in all four styles. Do you think any one is easier to read?

Most designers and editors also agree that type set in unusual shapes sacrifices readability. Circles and Christmas trees are better drawn than read—unless the message is unimportant, at which point you don't need type after all.

6. *Which of the column-edge styles on the next page would you choose for a textbook?*

_____

The ABC's of Typography

1 Printing is a method of multiplying a visual message, composed of words or symbols or pictures, so that many people, widely dispersed and without special equipment, can read it, either in whole or in part, simultaneously or at any time of their own choosing.
—Herbert Spencer

2 Printing is a method of multiplying a visual message, composed of words or symbols or pictures, so that many people, widely dispersed and without special equipment, can read it, either in whole or in part, simultaneously or at any time of their own choosing.
—Herbert Spencer

3 Printing is a method of multiplying a visual message, composed of words or symbols or pictures, so that many people, widely dispersed and without special equipment, can read it, either in whole or in part, simultaneously or at any time of their own choosing.
—Herbert Spencer

4 Printing is a method of multiplying a visual message, composed of words or symbols or pictures, so that many people, widely dispersed and without special equipment, can read it either in whole or in part, simultaneously or at any time of their own choosing.
—Herbert Spencer

Reverse Type. Body copy which is printed reverse, that is, with letters white on a dark background, is harder to read. That has been a printer's truism for years and has also been supported by typographic research. Small-size copy and italics which are reversed are particularly difficult to read. Larger-size display letters reversed out of a dark ground can hold their legibility. Compare the two type samples below:

As it has rolled down the centuries, Gutenberg's paper snowball has become an avalanche which now threatens to overwhelm us. —Herbert Spencer

For many years I have been trying to think out and check the criteria by which lettering should be judged. There are various definite factors: fitness for purpose, which includes legibility; fitness for the place and the material and process in question; competence of execution; judgment in details of design and spacing; sensitivity in delineation; feeling for individual letter character; originality. The relative importance of these factors varies with each particular job. —Nicolete Gray

Contrast. The easiest type to read in any family is the medium weight. Any large amount of type set all in bold will be very tiring. Copy set all in italic will be hard to read in mass because the lightface and delicate details are hard to discern. Both boldface and italic are good for contrast, but the value of contrast is lost if everything is set in bold or italic.

No matter how great the author's wisdom or how remarkable the printer's skill, unread print is merely a lot of paper and a little ink. The true economics of printing must be measured by how much is read and understood and not by how much is produced.

—Herbert Spencer

No matter how great the author's wisdom or how remarkable the printer's skill, unread print is merely a lot of paper and a little ink. The true economics of printing must be measured by how much is read and understood and not by how much is produced.
—Herbert Spencer

The ABC's of Typography

Review

None of these guidelines on legibility and readability have been carved in stone. They exist only as guides.

7. *When you are concerned with whether a letter is recognizable, are you concerned about legibility or readability?* _____
   When you are concerned with the process of scanning body copy, are you concerned about legibility or readability? _____
8. *When you design a logo like the script format used by Coca-Cola, what have you sacrificed for distinctiveness?* _____
9. *Is simplicity in the letter form a primary concern for legibility or for readability?* _____
10. *Which is thought to be more legible—sans serif or roman faces?*
    _____

    Which is thought to be easier to read for body copy—sans serif or roman faces? _____
11. *For the most legible display type, would you recommend upper- or lower-case letters?* _____
12. *Would you prefer display type which is letter spaced wide or set close?*
    _____

13. *What five factors determine the legibility of body copy?*

    1. _____   4. _____

    2. _____   5. _____

    3. _____
14. *What is the optimum line length for body copy?*
    _____

15. *Given a sample alphabet, how can you figure quickly an optimum line length?* _____
    _____

    Given 12-point type, what would you estimate your maximum line length would be? _____
16. *What is the range of optimum point sizes?* _____
    For these optimum type sizes, what is the range of appropriate leading? _____
17. *Which of these three specifications would yield the most readable body copy: (a) 20-pica line, 8-point type, 3 points leading? (b) 13-pica line, 14-point type, 1 point leading? (c) 14-pica line, 10-point type, 2 points leading?* _____

Chapter 9

Designing with Type

In many printed pieces, typography serves a purpose beyond that of simply conveying meaning via little black letters. Typography is an art form and it operates within an aesthetic environment. And while readability and the message are paramount, editors and designers cannot overlook the emotive power of type.

Functions of Typographic Design

In addition to the function of conveying a message, type has three other functions: establishing mood, attracting attention, and creating emphasis. These functions can be served only because of the tremendous range of type styles and sizes.

Establishing Mood. The wide range of ornamental faces provides effective tools for establishing various moods.

1. *Check your magazines and clip type samples which represent the following images:*
   Spring

   Elegant

   Ancient

Even the basic body-copy styles have emotive power. The romans, particularly Century Schoolbook, may remind you of your beginning readers. Sans serifs, in their simple skeletal style, are contemporary and bring forth images of skyscrapers, Danish furniture, computers, and other highly functional designs.

A book on medieval history could be painfully incongruous if it was set in Helvetica. A book on computers might look out of place set in Garamond.

2. *From the specimen list of nine typefaces, which would you use in an ad for a new "Whole Earth" catalog?*

   _____

   What face would you use for the annual report for an aeronautics company?

   _____

Mallard
Helvetica
Tiffany
Murray Hill
American Typewriter
Univers
SOUVENIR
Garamond Ultra
Oracle

Getting Attention: Typography is used to attract attention, by what Aaron Burns calls "graphic explosions." Typography is particularly important in publications and environments where the reader's attention is fragmented and distracted by a number of interfering items. This problem must be solved in billboards, road signs, and advertisements in magazines and newspapers.

The primary technique for getting attention is size. Big type in small quantities is instantly seen and usually assimilated. Big space draws attention. Big anything is effective, if you can use it.

Another technique is contrast, the chief typographic resource available to the designer. Contrast between parts of a design is achieved with such differences as large and small, thick against thin, dark with light. Contrast with nearby, often competing, designs is a recurring challenge. If you see that everything else is black and white, then use color. If everything around is big, then go small. If neighboring messages are filled with words and illustrations, then use a lot of white space. If the neighbors use white space, then fill your space with the message. Whatever you do in typographic design, it is most attention-getting if it is distinctive within its environment.

3. *Clip an advertisement which represents a good use of typographic contrast and include it here:*

The ABC's of Typography

Emphasis. Three typographic techniques are used to create emphasis: size, boldface (or color), and capitals.

If your body copy is set in 10-point, then set the subheads in boldface. Or use size: the subheads could be 12-point or all-caps.

TITLE

Subhead ·

Inset Head. Three ways are shown to indicate emphasis using the same typeface in the same size.

One suggestion regarding emphasis is to rank your typographic methods in order of their power to convey emphasis. How much you vary the levels of emphasis depends primarily upon the range of choices you have available. Generally you would want to increase the emphasis only by jumping to one higher level. For example you wouldn't need to make the subheads both 12-point and boldface. Keep the typographic progression logical with the steps in the organization of the content.

Thoughts on Form

Harmony. The discussion of functions and resources brings us to the question of mixing faces. Most typeface families have a wide variety within themselves—in both size and style. You can usually fit the mood, create emphasis, and attract attention—all within the same family.

If you do decide to mix faces, keep the mix limited. One face should predominate and the second serve as an accent. No more than two different typefaces should be used on a printed piece unless the purpose of the design is to create an eclectic feeling. Types in the same size range should be in the same family. Mix only faces which are widely separated in size.

The guidelines established by the legibility/readability discussion suggest ways to mix typefaces. Roman faces are found to be effective for body copy; sans serif is highly legible for display. This combination is common in newspapers. The opposite (sans serif for body and roman for display) is not so common and would distress the readability researchers, as well as your reader's eye.

4. *Cut out a variety of words from newspapers and magazines. Design a typographic montage on a subject of your choice with special attention to the order in which the design elements attract attention.*

Another aspect of harmony comes from matching the mood of the message to the nature of the audience. In the design of a message, the audience is sometimes forgotten—the old people, young people, women, truck drivers, architects, engineers, brides, athletes. They all have certain distinctive characteristics to which a message in their interests should be

earth moving equipment

run, Jane, run

your trousseau

fitted. For example, old people and beginning readers need large type in order to help them find the distinctive elements in the letters. Truck drivers on the highway need simple designs that can be read in an instant from a moving truck.

5. *In a magazine find an advertisement which is typographically oriented to a certain audience. Explain why the typographic design is directed that way.*

Another concern of harmony is to match the production methods with the type. Delicate and detailed typefaces with fine hairlines and serifs are best served by fine printing methods and quality paper which can reproduce the details. For example, the extreme contrast between the thick and thin strokes of Bodoni tends to blur on a fast-moving newspaper web press with its soft-textured and highly absorbent newsprint paper. Newsprint soaks up the ink like a blotter and, as on a blotter, the image spreads and the edges get fuzzy. Medium weight faces and faces with large x-heights and big counters are the easiest to reproduce on newsprint.

6. *See if you can find an example of an advertisement whose typography is poorly designed for the printing method used.*

Alignment. One of the small problems facing designers is the alignment of edges, especially horizontal edges. One abomination of designers is to try for an alignment and then just miss it slightly. This happens sometimes when typefaces with different x-heights are mixed in the same line. Then the critical horizontal line at the bottom of the x-height may not line up from face to face. This is to be avoided at all costs. Italic letters with their slant to the right also can be difficult to line up with anything. Even some upright letters won't cooperate. How can you visually align a headline beginning with an A or V with a copy block? Typographers live with these problems. They can't redesign the variation out of our letters or the readability and legibility would disappear.

One thing type users can do is adjust punctuation marks. In short blocks of copy, the edge alignment problem is easily disrupted by quotation marks, periods, commas, hyphens and dashes.

"Anybody can draw one letter; Some people can draw two; but it takes a designer to draw three."

—Harry Payne

Hanging such punctuation into the margin maintains the optical edge. This is a procedure recommended by most good designers. Study the sample shown here and see if you agree that "hung punctuation" is an improvement in alignment.

7. *See if you can find an example of hang punctuation in a contemporary magazine.*

Contemporary Design

Skilled calligraphers and hand letterers are still in demand—and a high price is paid for their work. Some of their work is displayed here.

Designed by Joel Kaden

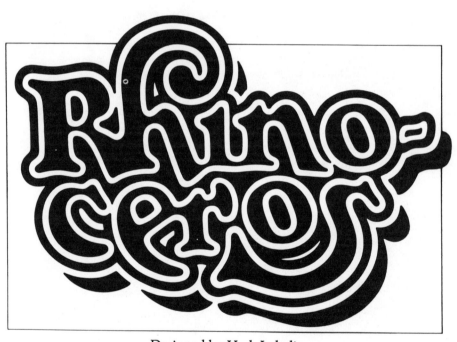

Designed by Herb Lubalin

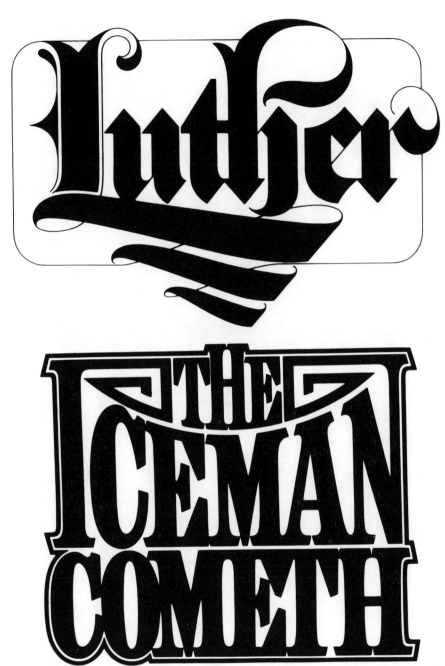

Designed by Herb Lubalin

8. *Using a brush, broad-point pen, or chisel-point magic marker, try lettering your favorite saying in one of the preceeding calligraphic styles.*

The ABC's of Typography

Typographic Design

Typographic design and the design of new type faces is a lively interest in graphic design. Here are some examples of the creativity of contemporary designers.

Designed by Ronald G. Thomas

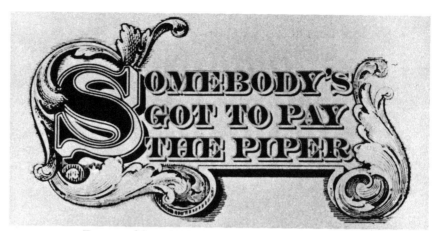

Designed by Harriet Winner and Dan Stewart

Designed by Dan Proctor and Tina Grant

9. *Design a typographic logotype for a museum or a travel agency (your choice). Draw the letters to style, use transfer type, or trace them as accurately as possible.*

New Typeface Designs

Surprisingly enough, more typefaces are being designed in these days than ever before. Some of these faces catch on and become classics, others are fads and fade quickly. Examine several recent alphabets devised by contemporary type designers:

Mexico Olympic, Wolf Magin, Mannheim

ABCDEFGHIJKLMNOPQR
STUVWXYZ

Gorilla, International Typeface Corp.

ABCDEFGHIJKLMMNOPQRR
STUVWXYZÆŒÇØaabcdefg?!
hhijklmmnnopqrsttuuvwxyz

A.K.I. Lines, International Typeface Corp.

ABCDEEFGHIJJKLM
NOPQRSTUVWXYYZ

Black Line, Wolf Magin, Mannheim

ABCDEFGHIJKLMNOP
QRSTUVWXYZ

Davida, Visual Graphics Corp.

AABCDEEFFGHIJKLMN
OPQRSTUVWXYZ

Paper Clip, Zipatone

The ABC's of Typography

Grouch, International Typeface Corp.

ABCDEFGHIJKKLMNNOPQ
RRSTUVWXYZ abcdefghijkk
lmnopqrstuvvwwxyyz

Ronda Light, International Typeface Corp.

ABCDEFGHIJKLMNOPQRSTUVWXYZ

abcdefghijklmnopqrstuvwxyz

Tiffany Medium, International Typeface Corp.

ABCDEFGHIJJKKLMNOPQRRS
TUVWXYZÇŒÆØabcdeefghijkkl
mnopqrstuvwxyz

Pierrot, Jantsch

ABCDEFGHIJKLMNOPQ
RSTUVWXYZ

Pinocchio, Neufville

ABCDEFGHIJKLMNOP
QRSTUVWXYZ

Neon, International Typeface Corp.

ABCDEFGHIJKLMNO
PQRSTUVWXYZ

Light Knight, Type Films of Chicago

ABCDEEFFGHHIJKLLMNOPQRS
TTUVWXYZaœbbccddeeffgghijjk
lmmnoppqqrrssttuuvuuwxyyz

Tushy, Type Films of Chicago

AÆBCCDEFGHIJKLMNOŒOP
QRSTUVWXYZ aæbcgdef
ghijklmnoœopqrsštuvwxyz

Cathedral, Type Films of Chicago

AABCDEFGHIJKKLMMNN
OPQRRSTUVWXYZ abcdefghi
jklmnopqrrstuvwxyz

Saxon, Type Films of Chicago

AAAABCDEEFFGHHHHHIJJKKKKKLL
MMMNNNOPPQRRRSTTUUUVWXYYZ

Happy Sid, Type Films of Chicago

ABCDEFGHIJKLMNOPQRST
UVWXYZ abcdefghijkllmn
opqrrstuvwxyz

The ABC's of Typography

10. *As your final project for this study of typography, design your own typeface. Write a one-page explanation of what you have created and state a rationale for the distinctive elements.*

Selected References

Books

Arnold, Edmund. *Ink on Paper.* 2nd ed. New York: Harper & Row, Publishers, 1972.

Bahr, Leonard F. *ATA Advertising Production Handbook.* 3rd ed. New York: Advertising Typographers Association of America, Inc., 1963.

Burns, Aaron. *Typography.* New York: Reinhold Publishing Corporation, 1951.

Craig, James. *Designing with Type.* New York: Watson-Guptill Publications, 1974.

Craig, James. *Production for the Graphic Designer.* New York: Watson-Guptill Publications, 1974.

Denman, Frank. *Shaping Our Alphabet.* New York: Alfred A. Knopf, 1955.

Gilliland, John. *Readability.* London: University of London Press, Ltd., 1972.

Goudy, Frederic W. *Typologia.* Berkeley and Los Angeles: University of California Press, 1940.

Hvistendahl, J. K., and Mary R. Kahl. *Roman v. Sans Serif Body Type: Readability and Reader Preference.* Washington, D.C.: American Newspaper Publishers Association News Research Bulletin.

Hurlburt, Allen. *Publication Design.* Rev. ed. Van Nostrand Reinhold Company, 1976.

Klare, George R. *The Measurement of Readability.* Ames, Iowa: Iowa State University Press, 1963.

Pocket Pal: A Graphic Arts Digest for Printers and Advertising Production Managers. 9th ed. New York: International Paper Company, 1966.

Jaspert, W. Pincus, W. Turner Berry, and A. F. Johnson. *The Encyclopedia of Type Faces.* 4th ed. New York: Barnes & Noble, 1970.

Nelson, Roy Paul. *The Design of Advertising.* 2nd ed. Dubuque, Iowa: Wm. C. Brown Company Publishers, 1973.

Nelson, Roy Paul. *Publication Design.* Dubuque, Iowa: Wm. C. Brown Company Publishers, 1972.

Rehe, Rolf F. *Typography: How to Make It Most Legible.* Indianapolis: Design Research Publications, 1974.

Ruegg, Ruedi, and Godi Frohlich. *Basic Typography.* Zurich, Switzerland: ABC Verlag, 1972.

Spencer, Herbert. *The Visible Word: Problems of Legibility*. 2nd ed. New York: Hastings House Publishers, 1969.

Tinker, Miles A. *Legibility of Print*. Ames, Iowa: Iowa State University Press, 1963.

White, Jan V. *Editing by Design*. New York: R. R. Bowker Company, 1974.

Zapf, Hermann. *About Alphabets: Some Marginal Notes on Type Design*. Cambridge, Mass.: The M.I.T. Press, 1970.

Periodicals

Art Direction, New York (monthly).

Communication Arts, Palo Alto, California (bimonthly).

Print, New York (bimonthly).

Typographers Digest, Philadelphia (quarterly).

U&lc, International Typeface Corporation, New York (quarterly).

Visible Language, The Cleveland Museum of Art, Cleveland, Ohio (quarterly).

Credits

Quotes

P. 29, Stanley Morison, *First Principles*, quoted by Max Caflisch; P. 35, Edward Rondthaler, "Geometric Formula for the Letter M," *U&lc*, 1:2; P. 47, Paul Doebler, "Word Processing, Typography, and the Gigo Principle," *U&lc*, 2:3, 1975; P. 110, Massin, "Letterforms, Signs, and Symbols," *U&lc*, 2:2, 1975; P. 111, John Dreyfus, "Typography—An Art Form that Enhances Communication," *U&lc*, 2:1, 1975; P. 112, Matthew Carter, "Typeface Design: Why and How Typefaces Differ," *U&lc*, 2:1, 1975; P. 114, Alvin Eisenman, "Letterforms, Signs, and Symbols," *U&lc*, 2:2, 1975; P. 115, Aaron Burns, *Typography*, New York: Reinhold Publishing Corp., 1961; P. 116, Edward M. Catich, "The Inscription-Making Process," *Father Catich and His Slates*, Wichita State University, 1974; P. 120, Aaron Burns, *Typography*, New York, Reinhold Publishing Corp.; P. 129, Edward Rondthaler, "How to Distinguish Typefaces," *U&lc*, 2:1, 1975; P. 140, Max Caflisch, "The Interdependence of Technique and Typography," *U&lc*, 2:1, 1974; P. 141, Ruedi Ruegg and Godi Fohlich, *Basic Typography*, Switzerland ABC Edition Zurich, 1972; P. 144, Herbert Spencer, *The Visible Word*, New York: Hastings House, 1969; P. 146, Nicolete Gray, "Lettering and Society," *U&lc*, 1:2, 1974; P. 146, Herbert Spencer, *The Visible Word*, New York: Hastings House, 1969; P. 157, Harry Payne quoted in "How to Distinguish Typefaces" by Edward Rondthaler, *U&lc*, 2:1, 1975.

Illustrations

P. 24, Arthur Baker, *Calligraphy*, Dover Publications, Inc.; P. 31, Western Typesettting Photomodifications; From *Creativity 4*, Art Direction Book Co., New York; P. 24, Lubalin, Smith and Carnase; P. 95, Dan Proctor and Tina Grant; P. 135, Murray Smith and Michael Doret; P. 158, Joel Kadden; P. 158, Herb Lubalin; P. 159, Herb Lubalin; P. 161, Ronald G. Thomas; P. 162, Harriet Winner and Dan Stewart; P. 162, Dan Proctor and Tina Grant.

Production

This book was set in 10 on 12 Palatino by The Book Press, Brattleboro, Vermont.
The headlines are in 14 and 24 point Americana.

Appendix 1

Answers to Exercises

Answers are given here for those exercises that involve questions of fact or require calculations.

Chapter 1: 14A—lower, upright, small, thick and thin, angled, slanted. **14B**—lower, upright, large, thick and thin, angled, slanted. **14C**—lower, italic, small, thick and thin, angled, slanted. **14D** lower, upright, large, thick and thin (slight), sans, upright. **14E**—upper, upright, unknown, thick and thin, angled, upright and slanted (compare the C and O).

Chapter 3: 1—½ inch, 18 lines. **2**—18 picas, 1 pica. **3**—2 picas, 24 pts, 12 pts. **4**—3 ems, 35 pts, 3 picas. **5**—enlarged letter is bigger and wider, strokes are narrower. **6**—21, 2.1, 50, 5.0, 4.2×2.1. **7**—10 pt. **8**—12 lines, 19 lines. **9**—2 lines 1 em. **10**—13 picas, 5.47 cm.

Chapter 4: 1—12 pts, 72 pts, 1 inch, 2.52 cm. **2**—36 picas, 36 lines. **3**—a, b. **4**—2 pts, 1 pt. **5**—VA, LV, VE, tw, we. **6**—round letters together and tall vertical letters together. **7**—between lb, il, ll, lb, il, ll; between sc, ch, ho, oo, ol, bo, oo, ok, ly. **8**—li, it, tl; ma, am, mm, ma. **9**—either; definitely 2 pts. **10**—small X height. **11**—7 lines. **12**— circles between EV, VE, FA, FR, LL, LY, LA; diagonals between NE, HI, IL, ND. **13**— + between Il, ll, ll; = between An, Ov, er, rl, ly, ra, at, te, ed, Ba, oo.

Chapter 5: 2—c, 2, 3, 5, 7, 8; X, 1, 4, 6. **3**—condensed. **4**—extended. **6**—2, 6, 8; 5. **7**—3, 6. **8.1**—width; a, condensed; b, medium; c, extended; **8.2**—weight; a, light; b, medium; c, bold. **8.3**—posture; a, roman; b, italic. **9**—c, 3; X, 8; italic, 5; bold, 3, 7, 8, 9, 11; light, 2, 10. **16**—2, 4, 6, 7, 10; 1, 3, 8, 9; 5. **17**—2, 3, 5, 7. **21**—2, 5, 8; 4, 6, 9, 10; 1, 3, 7. **22.1**—black letters. **22.2**—scripts and cursives. **22.3**—ornamentals; a, mood; b, imitative. **22.4**—romans; a, old style; b, transitional; c, modern. **22.5**—sans serif. **22.6**—contemporary serifs; a, square, b, rounded; c, inscribed. **23**—7; 2; 3; 4; 5; 1; 12; 8; :6; 9.

Chapter 6: 1—Univers Light, 31.6 or 32, 28.9 or 29.2. **2**—3.53, 2.6, 1.77, 2.59. **3**—47, 18, 2.61. **4**—2.95, 71. **5**—2.03, 37, 42. **6**—24, 4, 18. **7**— 3.03, 55. **8**—19 picas wide, 6 picas deep. **9**—2.5, 47.5 or 48. **10**—6 lines. **11**—72 pts, 7.2 or 7 lines. **12**—56 characters, 12 lines. **13**— 2.95 cpp, 18 picas, 53 characters, 13 picas, 38 characters. **14**—3 of 18, 17, 15, 14, 13½, 13, 13, 13½, 14, 15, 17, 3 of 18. **15**—3 of 53, 50, 44, 41, 40, 38, 38, 40, 41, 44, 50, 3 of 53. **16**—53 characters, 4 lines. **17**—1.38, 16 picas, 18 picas. **18**—14 picas. **19**—25 units, 21 characters; 18½ units, 21 characters. **21**—13, 27. **22**—28, 22½, 14, 10½. **23**—16 picas, 25½ picas. **24**—18 pt.

Chapter 7: 1—12 on 12, 12 on 16. **2**—18/10 on 12 Century. **3**—15/12 on 14 Baskerville, ragged right. **4**—indent 3 lines 3 ems. **5**—(in points) 8, 4, 2, 4, 2, 4, 2, 8, 4, 2, 4, 2, 4, 2. **7**— +1 between MI, IN, NI, IT, IK: −1 between WN, OK: −2 between TO, OW, LO, PA, AC, TO, OY. **8**— leading instructions. **11**—faces/races, sans/sens, detail/detale, Univers/Universe, had to *before* make, repeatedly/repetedly, elements in the design of a *repeated* (delete one phrase), complete/complate.

Chapter 8: 1—Helvetica. **2**—Garamond. **3**—2. **7**—legibility, legibility. **8**—legibility. **9**—legibility. **10**—sans serif, roman. **11**—lower-case. **12**— set close. **13**—design, type size, line length, leading, column edges. **14**—18 to 24 picas. **15**—1½ X lower-case alphabet, 24 picas. **16**—9 to 12 point, 1 to 4 points. **17**—c.

Appendix 2

Metric Conversion Tables

Metric to Points and Inches

CM	MM	Pts.	Picas	Inches
	1	2.8529	.2377	.03937
	2	5.71	.48	.08
	3	8.56	.71	.12
	4	11.41	.95	.16
	5	14.26	1.19	.20
	6	17.12	1.43	.24
	7	19.97	1.66	.28
	8	22.82	1.90	.31
	9	25.68	2.14	.35
1	10	28.53	2.38	.39
	11	31.38	2.61	.43
	12	34.23	2.85	.47
	13	37.09	3.09	.51
	14	39.94	3.33	.55
	15	42.29	3.57	.59
	16	45.65	3.80	.63
	17	48.50	4.04	.67
	18	51.35	4.28	.71
	19	54.21	4.52	.75
2	20	57.21	4.75	.79
	21	59.91	4.99	.83
	22	62.76	5.23	.87
	23	65.61	5.47	.91
	24	68.47	5.71	.95
	25	71.32	5.94	.99
	26	74.18	6.18	1.02
	27	77.03	6.42	1.06
	28	79.88	6.66	1.10
	29	82.73	6.89	1.14
3	30	85.36	7.13	1.18
	31	88.44	7.37	1.22
	32	91.29	7.61	1.26
	33	94.15	7.85	1.30
	34	97.00	8.07	1.34
	35	99.85	8.31	1.38
	36	102.70	8.56	1.42
	37	105.56	8.80	1.46
	38	108.41	9.03	1.50
	39	111.26	9.27	1.54
4	40	114.12	9.51	1.57
5	50	142.65	11.89	1.97
6	60	171.17	14.26	2.36
7	70	199.70	16.64	2.76
8	80	228.23	19.02	3.15
9	90	256.76	21.40	3.54
10	100	285.29	23.77	3.94

Points to Metric

Picas	Points	MM	Inch
	1	.35052	.0138
	2	.70	.03
	3	1.05	.04
	4	1.40	.06
	5	1.75	.07
	6	2.10	.08
	7	2.45	.10
	8	2.80	.11
	9	3.15	.12
	10	3.51	.14
	11	3.86	.15
1	12	4.21	.17
	13	4.56	.18
	14	4.91	.19
	15	5.26	.21
	16	5.61	.22
	17	5.96	.24
	18	6.31	.25
	19	6.66	.26
	20	7.01	.28
	21	7.36	.29
	22	7.71	.30
	23	8.06	.32
2	24	8.41	.33
	25	8.76	.35
	26	9.11	.36
	27	9.46	.37
	28	9.81	.39
	29	10.17	.40
	30	10.52	.41
	31	10.87	.43
	32	11.22	.44
	33	11.57	.45
	34	11.92	.47
	35	12.27	.49
3	36	12.62	.50
	37	12.97	.51
	38	13.32	.52
	39	13.67	.54
	40	14.02	.55
	41	14.37	.57
	42	14.72	.58
	43	15.07	.59
	44	15.42	.61
	45	15.77	.62
	46	16.12	.64
	47	16.47	.65
4	48	16.82	.66
5	60	21.03	.83
6	72	25.30	.99
7	84	29.44	1.16
8	96	33.65	1.33
10	120	42.06	1.66

Characters Per Pica for Selected Typefaces

CHARACTER COUNT CHART (CPP)

Adapted from the AD Copyfitter

The following character counts are given for common sizes of body types. The counts are based on the faces supplied by the type foundries identified in the code below. If you are using a type face from a different machine than the one listed, you might want to check a sample specimen to see if your equipment sets the characters at the same count. This is particularly true of photocomposition equipment in which widths may differ even when supplied by the same manufacturer.

	Code for Type Companies
A/C	— Amsterdam Continental
ATF	— American Type Founders
Bal	— Baltimore
B	— Bauer
CG	— Compugraphic
Eur	— European
F	— Fotosetter
I	— Intertype
ITC	— International Typeface Corp.
Li	— Linotype (Mergenthaler)
Lud	— Ludlow
M	— Monotype
K-S	— Klingspor-Stempel
S-B	— Stephenson-Blake
Si	— Simoncini
T	— Tape operation

Alternate Gothic No. 1 (1) 8-4.39;
10-3.8; 12-3.29; 14-2.8; 18-2.35;
24-1.78

Antique No. 1 & It. (I & Li) 6-3.56;
7-3.19; 8-2.80; 9-2.56; 10-2.45;
12-2.04; 14-1.78; 18-1.45; 24-1.12

Avant Garde Gothic Ex. Light (ITC)
8-3.1; 10-2.49; 12-2.23; 14-1.87;
18-1.51

Avant Garde Gothic Med. (ITC) 8-3.1;
10-2.49; 12-2.2; 14-1.86; 18-1.51

Avant Garde Gothic Demi (ITC) 8-2.95;
10-2.39; 12-2.1; 14-1.77; 18-1.44

Avant Garde Gothic Bold (ITC) 8-2.9;
10-2.35; 12-2.07; 14-1.73; 18-1.41

Avant Garde Med. Cond. (ITC) 8-3.53;
10-2.95; 12-2.45; 14-2.17; 18-1.7

Baskerville & It. (Li) 6-3.83; 7-3.68;
8-3.19; 9-2.94; 10-2.68; 11-2.45;
12-2.25; 14-2.04; 16-1.78

Baskerville Bold & It. (Li) 6-3.83;
7-3.56; 8-3.2; 9-2.89; 10-2.61; 11-2.42;
12-2.28; 14-1.98

Bernhard Gothic Ex Heavy (ATF)
12-2.18; 14-1.81; 18-1.44; 24-1.07

Bernhard Gothic Heavy (ATF) 8-3.34;
10-2.73; 12-2.41; 14-2.03; 18-1.62;
24-1.21

Bernhard Gothic Light (ATF) 6-4.3;
8-3.65; 10-2.95; 12-2.61; 14-2.15;
18-1.77; 24-1.31

Bernhard Gothic Light It. (ATF) 6-4.57;
8-3.82; 10-3.13; 12-2.72; 14-2.32;
18-1.88; 24-1.41

Bernhard Gothic Medium (ATF) 6-4.26;
8-3.75; 10-2.96; 12-2.64; 14-2.29;
18-1.75; 24-1.33

Bernhard Gothic Medium Cond. (ATF)
12-3.35; 14-2.74; 18-2.19; 24-1.68

Bernhard Gothic Medium It. (ATF)
6-4.26; 8-3.61; 10-2.94; 12-2.61;
14-2.17; 18-1.74; 24-1.31

Bernhard Modern (ATF) 8-3.56;
10-3.05; 12-2.56; 14-2.14; 18-1.78;
24-1.34

Bodoni & It. (Li) 6-3.9; 7-3.4; 8-3.08;
9-2.83; 10-2.55; 11-2.45; 12-2.37;
14-2.14; 18-1.68; 24-1.31; 30-1.09

Bodoni Bold & It. (Li) 6-3.68; 7-3.31;
8-2.94; 9-2.56; 10-2.45; 11-2.35;
12-2.14; 14-1.92; 18-1.54; 21-1.34;
24-1.23; 30-1.02; 36-.87

Bookman & It. (Li) 6-3.53; 7-3.28;
8-3.05; 9-2.83; 10-2.55; 11-2.38;
12-2.23; 14-1.89

Bookman O. S. (ATF) 6-3.59; 8-3.18;
10-2.67; 12-2.24; 14-1.89; 18-1.42;
24-.95

Bulmer (M) 6-3.75; 7-3.63; 8-3.33;
9-3.06; 10-2.83; 11-2.65; 12-2.53;
14-2.23; 16-1.98; 18-1.75; 18#2-1.45;
24-1.45

Bulmer It. (M) 6-4.18; 7-3.46; 8-3.5;
9-3.22; 10-2.98; 11-2.78; 12-2.66;
14-2.37; 16-2.14; 18-1.9; 18#2-1.45;
24-1.45

Cairo (I) 6-3.57; 8-3.03; 10-2.55;
12-2.09; 14-1.78; 18-1.46; 24-1.13

Cairo It. (I) 6-3.53; 8-2.97; 10-2.46;
12-.; 14-1.71; 18-1.4

Cairo Bold (I) 6-3.52; 8-3.05; 10-2.58;
12-2.07; 14-1.78; 18-1.4; 24-1.11

Cairo Bold Cond. (I) 8-3.45; 10-2.97;
12-2.46; 14-2.11; 18-1.76; 24-1.42

Caledonia w It. & S. C. (Li) 6-3.55;
7-3.30; 8-3.08; 9-2.83; 10-2.59;
11-2.43; 12-2.30; 14-2.05; 18-1.52;
24-1.22

Caledonia Bold w It & S. C. (Li) 6-3.50;
7-3.28; 8-3.08; 9-2.80; 10-2.58;
11-2.41; 12-2.27; 14-2.02; 18-1.51;
24-1.22

California (CG) 8-3.22; 10-2.61;
12-2.19; 14-1.71; 18-1.44

Caslon w It. & S. C. (Li) 7-3.45; 8-3.10;
9-2.95; 10-2.78; 11-2.4; 12-2.2;
14-1.95; 18-1.55; 24-1.15; 30-.95

Caslon No. 137 w It. & S. C. (Li) 7-3.6;
8-3.23; 9-2.9; 10-2.6; 11-2.41; 12-2.24

Caslon Antique (ATF) 8-3.43; 10-3.31;
12-2.94; 18-1.78

Caslon Bold (Lud) 6-3.26; 8-2.77;
10-2.45; 12-2.02; 14-1.71; 18-1.31;
24-1.02

Caslon Heavy (ATF) 6-3.28; 8-2.89;
10-2.29; 12-.; 14-1.66; 18-1.31;
24-1.04

Caslon Old Face w It. & S. C. (Li)
6-4.15; 8-3.45; 9-3.15; 10-3.03;
11-2.75; 11½-2.53; 12-2.42; 14-2.29;
18-2.; 21-1.65; 24-1.51; 30-1.08;
36-.85

Century Bold w It. (Li) 6-3.56; 7-3.05;
8-2.9; 10-2.35; 11-2.25; 12-2.08;
14-1.75; 18-1.53; 24-1.17; 30-.96;
36-.77

Century Expanded w It. & S. C. (Li)
4-4.1; 5-4.; 6-3.43; 7-3.13; 8-2.83;
9-2.63; 10-2.4; 11-2.31; 12-2.15;
14-1.81; 18-1.53; 24-1.13

Century Schoolbook & It. (I) 6-3.71;
7-3.22; 8-2.89; 9-2.69; 10-2.5; 11-2.35;
12-2.14; 14-1.79; 18-1.44

Century Schoolbook & Bold (I) 6-3.67;
7-3.2; 8-2.87; 9-2.67; 10-2.5; 11-2.32;
12-2.14; 14-1.79

Cheltenham w It. & S. C. (Li) 8-3.4;
9-3.13; 10-2.93; 11-2.67; 12-2.5;
14-2.29; 18-1.78; 20-1.75; 24-1.42;
30-1.22; 36-1.04

Cheltenham Bold (Lud) 6-3.6; 8-3.05;
10-2.42; 12-2.21; 14-1.93; 18-1.46;
24-1.12

Cheltenham Bold Cond. w It. (Li)
6-4.15; 8-3.43; 10-2.88; 12-2.54;
14-2.23; 18-1.8; 24-1.48; 30-1.19;
36-1.03

Cheltenham Medium & It. No. 186 (M)
5-4.52; 6-3.83; 7-3.43; 8-3.19; 9-3.05;
10-2.68; 11-2.45; 12-2.25; 14-1.92;
18-1.54; 24-1.23

Cheltenham O. S. (ATF) 6-4.57; 8-3.85;
10-3.19; 12-2.72; 14-2.25; 18-1.81;
24-1.42

Cheltenham Bold Extended (ATF)
6-2.66; 8-2.31; 10-1.79; 12-1.61;
14-1.34; 18-1.07; 24-.84

Cheltenham Wide & Bold (Li) 6-3.43;
8-3.05; 10-2.56; 12-2.25; 14-1.78

Clarendon + Bold (Li) 7-2.85; 8-2.63;
9-2.35; 10-2.17

Clarendon (Craw) (ATF) 8-2.4; 10-2.0;
12-1.7; 14-1.5; 18-1.1; 24-.91

Cloister w It. & S. C. (Li) 6-3.95; 8-3.4;
10-3.05; 11-2.9; 12-2.7; 14-2.44;
18-1.97; 24-1.46; 30-1.24; 36-1.07

Cloister Bold w It. (Li) 6-3.6; 8-3.08;
10-2.66; 12-2.45; 14-2.22; 18-1.74;
24-1.37; 30-1.14; 36-.96

Cloister Wide w Cloister Bold (Li)
6-3.6; 8-3.08; 10-2.67; 12-2.45;
14-2.22

Cooper Black (ATF) 6-2.95; 8-2.6;
10-2.03; 12-1.75; 14-1.42; 18-1.09;
24-.83

Cooper Black It. (ATF) 6-3.37; 8-2.78;
10-2.2; 12-1.89; 14-1.58; 18-1.2; 24-.91

Craw Modern (ATF) 6-2.3; 8-1.9;
10-1.7; 12-1.4; 14-1.2; 18-.96; 24-.70

Craw Modern Bold (ATF) 6-2.0; 8-1.8;
10-1.5; 12-1.2; 14-1.1; 18-.85; 24-.64

Erbar Light Cond. w Erbar Bold Cond.
(Li) 8-3.9; 10-3.4; 12-3.2; 14-2.73;
18-2.15; 24-1.75

Folio Bold Cond. (B) 8-4.05; 10-3.4; 11-3.17; 12-2.85; 14-2.55; 16-2.22; 18-1.99; 24-1.6

Folio Bold Extended (B) 8-2.43; 10-1.99; 12-1.56; 14-1.33; 16-1.08; 18-.94; 24-.76

Folio Book (B) 8-3.84; 10-3.17; 12-2.53; 14-2.14; 16-1.77; 18-1.56; 24-1.26

Folio Demibold (B) 8-3.84; 10-3.14; 12-2.49; 14-2.11; 16-1.74; 18-1.53; 24-1.24

Folio Light (B) 6-4.56; 8-3.6; 10-3.1; 11-2.73; 12-2.5; 14-2.18; 16-1.77; 18-1.59; 24-1.27; 30-1.09

Folio Light Condensed (B) 8-4.56; 10-3.72; 12-3.03; 14-2.63; 16-2.16; 18-1.88; 24-1.59

Folio Medium (B) 6-4.44; 8-3.6; 10-3.05; 11-2.72; 12-2.45; 14-2.29; 16-1.8; 18-1.59; 24-1.27; 30-1.07

Folio Medium Condensed (B) 8-4.11; 10-3.93; 12-3.08; 14-2.63; 16-2.02; 18-1.86; 24-1.59

Folio Medium Extended (B) 8-2.9; 10-2.38; 11-2.15; 12-2.01; 14-1.72; 16-1.37; 18-1.21; 24-1.; 30-.81; 36-.69

Franklin Gothic Cond. (ATF) 6-3.48; 8-3.03; 10-2.4; 12-2.21; 14-1.87; 18-1.51; 24-1.2

Franklin Gothic Ex Cond. (ATF) 6-4.12; 8-3.6; 10-2.96; 12-2.76; 14-2.31; 18-1.92; 24-1.54

Franklin Gothic It. (ATF) 5-3.80; 6-3.15; 8-2.7; 10-2.07; 12-1.84; 14-1.52; 18-1.22; 24-.96

Franklin Gothic Wide (ATF) 6-2.56; 8-2.15; 10-1.71; 12-1.54; 14-1.3; 18-1.

Fritz Quadrata (ITC) 8-3.15; 10-2.55; 12-2.23; 14-2; 18-1.54

Fritz Quadrata Bold (ITC) 8-3.09; 10-2.46; 12-2.10; 14-1.83; 18-1.43

Futura Bold (I) 6-3.64; 8-3.11; 10-2.43; 12-1.98; 14-1.75; 18-1.41; 24-1.04

Futura Bold Cond. (I) 6-4.82; 8-3.72; 10-3.11; 12-2.77; 14-2.48; 18-1.9; 24-1.61; 30-1.33

Futura Demibold (I) 6-4.02; 8-3.49; 9-3.05; 10-2.59; 11-2.54; 12-2.3; 14-2.01; 18-1.52; 24-1.23; 36-.70

Futura Demibold Oblique (I) 6-4; 8-3.49; 9-3.05; 10-2.59; 11-2.54; 12-2.3; 14-2.; 18-1.52; 24-1.23

Futura Light (I) 6-4.44; 8-3.76; 10-3.09; 12-2.59; 14-2.26

Futura Medium (I) 6-4.22; 8-3.6; 10-2.87; 12-2.42; 14-2.11; 16-1.76; 18-1.61

Futura Medium Cond. (I) 8-4.82; 10-3.72; 12-3.11; 14#1-2.77; 14#2-2.48; 18-1.9; 24-1.64; 30-1.33

Garamond & It. (I) 6-3.93; 7-3.67; 8-3.37; 9-3.18; 10-2.95; 11-2.7; 12-2.59; 14-2.3; 18-1.77; 24-1.38

Garamond Bold & It. (I) 6-3.75; 7-3.43; 8-3.19; 9-2.91; 10-2.75; 11-2.54; 12-2.42; 14-2.17; 18-1.61; 24-1.21

Goudy Bold & It. (I) 6-3.69; 8-3.03; 10-2.48; 12-2.16; 14-1.78; 18-1.47; 24-1.13

Goudy O. S. & It. (ATF) 6-4.35; 8-3.56; 10-3.05; 12-2.56; 14-2.14; 18-1.78; 24-1.34

Helios Light (CG) 8-3.26; 10-2.67; 12-2.25; 14-1.84; 18-1.47

Helios Bold (CG) 8-2.97; 10-2.43; 12-2.06; 14-1.68; 18-1.34

Helvetica + Bold (Li) 6-3.84; 7-3.42; 8-3.08; 9-2.71; 10-2.47; 12-2.07; 14-1.80

Helvetica Bold + It. (Li) 6-3.84; 7-3.39; 8-3.05; 9-2.64; 10-2.46; 11-2.26; 12-2.06; 14-1.80

Helvetica w It. (Li) 6-3.50; 7-3.30; 8-3.03; 9-2.66; 10-2.45; 11-2.26; 12-2.07; 14-1.80

Helvetica w Semi-Bold (Li) 6-3.50; 7-3.33; 8-3.02; 9-2.70; 10-2.45; 12-2.15

Janson w It. & S. C. (Li) 8-3.03; 9-2.75; 10-2.57; 11-2.44; 12-2.33; 14-2.11

Jenson & It. (Li) 8-3.05; 10-2.68; 12-2.25; 14-1.92

Kabel Bold (A/C) 6-4.; 8-3.19; 10-2.8; 12-2.56; 14-2.25; 18-2.04; 24-1.54

Kabel Bold It. (A/C) 6-3.83; 8-3.19; 10-2.8; 12-2.35; 14-2.14; 18-1.92; 24-1.45

Kabel Ex Bold (A/C) 6-3.43; 8-2.68; 10-2.04; 12-1.78; 14-1.54; 18-1.45

Kabel Light (A/C) 6-4.19; 8-3.43; 10-2.94; 12-2.56; 14-2.25; 18-2.04; 24-1.54

Kabel Light It. (A/C) 6-4.35; 8-3.68; 10-3.05; 12-2.68; 14-2.35; 18-2.14;

Kaufman Bold (Allow for Swashes) (ATF) 10-2.85; 12-2.58; 14-2.32; 18-1.77; 24-1.37

Kaufman Script (Allow for Swashes) (ATF) 10-3.10; 12-2.84; 14-2.54; 18-1.94;

Korinna (ITC) 8-3.35; 10-2.9; 12-2.33; 14-2.13; 18-1.67

Korinna Bold (ITC) 8-3.3; 10-2.66; 12-2.3; 14-2.07; 18-1.62

Korinna Ex. Bold (ITC) 8-3; 10-2.43; 12-2.07; 14-1.86; 18-1.46

Korrina Heavy (ITC) 8-2.7; 10-2.23; 12-1.89; 14-1.67; 18-1.3

Lydian & It. (I) 8-3.56; 10-2.87; 12-2.34; 14-2.05; 18-1.67; 24-1.27

Lydian Bold & It. (I) 8-3.42; 10-2.78; 12-2.25; 14-1.99; 18-1.62; 24-1.22

Lydian Bold Cond. It. (ATF) 10-3.3; 12-2.7; 14-2.3; 18-1.9; 24-1.5

Mallard, Bold & Ital (CG) 8-2.94; 10-2.54; 12-2.13; 14-1.78; 18-1.41

Melior (A/C) 6-3.67; 8-3.32; 8#2-3.05; 10-2.79; 12-2.54; 12#2-2.24; 14-2.03; 18-1.78; 24-1.33

Melior Bold Cond. (A/C) 12-2.54; 12#2-2.14; 14-1.91; 18-1.64; 24-1.33

Melior It. (A/C) 6-3.67; 8-3.32; 8#2-3.05; 10-2.79; 12-2.54; 12#2-2.24; 14-1.91; 18-1.64; 24-1.23

Melior Semi-Bold (A/C) 6-3.67; 8-3.32; 8#2-3.05; 10-2.79; 12-2.54; 12#2-2.24; 14-1.91; 18-1.64; 24-1.23

Memphis Medium w It. & S. C. (Li) 6-3.38; 8-3.18; 9-2.78; 10-2.5; 12-2.09; 14-1.87; 18-1.78; 18-1.51; 24-1.12; 30-.95; 36-.83

News Gothic & Bold (CG) 8-3.31; 10-2.61; 12-2.25; 14-1.77; 18-1.46

News Gothic Cond. (CG) 8-3.77; 10-3.17; 12-2.74; 18-1.77

Newtext (ITC) 8-2.95; 10-2.37; 12-2.03; 14-1.83; 18-1.44

Newtext It., & Demi (ITC) 8-2.9; 10-2.35; 12-2.01; 14-1.79; 18-1.39

Optima w It. (Li) 6-3.60; 7-3.30; 8-3.10; 9-2.80; 10-2.50.

Optima w Semi-Bold (Li) 6-3.65; 7-3.25; 8-3.1; 9-2.80; 10-2.50.

Oracle, Bold & Ital. (CG) 8-3.18; 10-2.57; 12-2.16; 14-1.8; 18-1.43

Paladium, Bold & Ital. (CG) 8-3.14; 10-2.67; 12-2.22; 14-1.78; 18-1.48

Palatino (K-S) 6-4.35; 8-4.; 8#2-3.32; 10-3.05; 12-2.67; 12#2-2.35; 14-2.03; 18-1.78; 20-1.33

Palatino It. (K-S) 6-4.89; 8-4.55; 8#2-4.; 10-3.54; 12-3.32; 12#2-2.79; 14-2.44; 18-2.14; 20-1.78; 24-1.44

Record Gothic Cond. (Lud) 6-4.6; 8-3.67; 10-3.13; 12-2.87; 14-2.44;

Appendix 3: Characters per Pica for Selected Typefaces

18-1.93; 24-1.51
Record Gothic Extended (Lud) 6-3.288; 8-2.533; 10-2.085; 12-1.781; 14-1.507; 18-1.179; 24-.905
Record Gothic Heavy Medium-Extended (Lud) 6-3.32; 8-2.39; 10-2.11; 12-1.79; 14-1.53; 18-1.21; 24-.93
Rondo (Allow for Swashes) (ATF) 10-3.05; 12-2.7; 18-2.; 24-1.6; 24#2-1.4
Scotch Roman (ATF) 6-3.61; 8-3.18; 10-2.85; 11-2.7; 12-2.26; 14-1.87; 18-1.45; 24-1.12
Serif Gothic Light (ITC) 8-3.3; 10-2.7; 12-2.33; 14-2.10; 18-1.65
Serif Gothic & Bold (ITC) 8-3.15; 10-2.57; 12-2.23; 14-2.01; 18-1.56
Serif Gothic Heavy (ITC) 8-3.1; 10-2.52; 12-2.17; 14-1.95; 18-1.57
Souvenir Light (ITC) 8-3.4; 10-2.8; 12-2.37; 14-2.23; 18-1.66
Souvenir & It. (ITC) 8-3.20; 10-2.63; 12-2.23; 14-2.05; 18-1.53
Souvenir Demi (ITC) 8-3; 10-2.43; 12-2.07; 14-1.93; 18-1.41
Souvenir Bold (ITC) 8-2.8; 10-2.3; 12-1.95; 14-1.78; 18-1.33
Spartan Black (ATF) 6-3.32; 8-3.08; 10-2.39; 12-1.99; 14-1.75; 18-1.36; 24-1.07
Spartan Black Cond. (ATF) 10-2.9; 12-2.65; 14-2.43; 18-1.97; 24-1.55
Spartan Book w It. S. C. (Li) 6-3.63; 8-3.35; 9-2.98; 10-2.63; 11-2.44; 12-2.33; 14-2.11; 18-1.6; 24-1.29
Spartan Book w Heavy (Li) 5½-3.65; 6-3.63; 8-3.35; 9-2.95; 10-2.6; 11-2.43; 12-2.31; 14-2.1; 18-1.59; 24-1.29
Spartan Medium (ATF) 6-3.84; 8-3.66; 10-2.92; 12-2.5; 14-2.16; 18-1.68; 24-1.39
Stymie Bold & It. (ATF) 6-3.31; 8-2.8; 10-2.25; 12-2.04; 14-1.65; 18^2-1.45; 18^1-1.34; 24-1.01
Stymie Light (ATF) 6-3.79; 8-3.21; 10-2.41; 10#2-2.76; 12-2.18; 14-1.81; 18-1.43; 18#2-1.61; 24-1.15
Tempo Bold (Lud) 6-4.02; 8-3.34; 10-2.61; 12-2.31; 14-1.95; 18-1.47; 24-1.07
Tempo Bold Cond. (Lud) 6-5.34; 8-4.12; 10-3.38; 12-2.94; 14-2.52; 18-1.95; 24-1.45
Tempo Heavy (Lud) 6-3.6; 8-2.81; 10-2.43; 12-2.01; 14-1.79; 18-1.31;

24-.99
Tempo Heavy Cond. (Lud) 6-4.89; 8-3.82; 10-3.11; 12-2.80; 14-2.39; 18-1.98; 24-1.48; 30-1.23
Tempo Light (Lud) 6-4.73; 8-3.79; 10-3.29; 12-2.75; 14-2.33; 18-1.76; 24-1.29
Tempo Medium (Lud) 6-4.47; 8-3.56; 10-3.04; 12-2.75; 14-2.24; 18-1.72; 24-1.29
Tiffany Light (ITC) 8-3.15; 10-2.55; 12-2.17; 14-1.9; 18-1.47
Tiffany & Demi (ITC) 8-2.95; 10-2.4; 12-2.07; 14-1.77; 18-1.39
Tiffany Heavy (ITC) 8-2.56; 10-2.10; 12-1.77; 14-1.49; 18-1.34
Times Roman w It. & S. C. (Li) 5½-3.8; 6-.36; 7-3.3; 8-3.08; 9-2.85; 10-2.69; 11-2.5; 12-2.33; 14-2.15
Times Roman Bold (Li) 5½-4.07; 6-3.8; 7-3.40; 8-3.14; 9-2.90; 10-2.73; 11-2.53; 12-2.31; 14-2.07
Trade Gothic Cond. w Bold (Li) 6-3.85; 7-3.65; 8-3.53; 9-3.3; 10-3.13; 11-2.98; 12-2.83; 14-2.44; 18-2.; 24-1.6
Trade Gothic Extended w Bold (Li) 6-2.8; 7-2.55; 8-2.35; 9-2.2; 10-2.05; 11-1.9; 12-1.75; 14-1.5
Trade Gothic Light w It. (Li) 6-3.35; 7-3.2; 8-3.0; 9-2.75; 10-2.55; 11-2.4; 12-2.25; 14-2.0
20th Century Ex Bold No. 603 (M) 6-3.69; 8-3.19; 9-2.66; 10-2.4; 11-2.14; 12-2.01
20th Century Bold No. 604 (M) 6-4.; 8-3.48; 9-3.05; 10-2.61; 11-2.35; 12-2.26; 14-2.01; 16-1.64; 18-1.53
20th Century Light No. 606 (M) 6-4.68; 8-3.81; 10-3.08; 12-2.61; 14-2.26; 16-1.91; 18-1.7; 24-1.33
20th Century Medium No. 605 (M) 6-4.68; 8-3.66; 9-3.32; 10-2.94; 11-2.67; 12-2.44; 14-2.09; 16-1.78; 18-1.62; 24-1.23
Univers 45 (ATF) 6-3.9; 8-3.2; 10-2.8; 12-2.3; 14-2.0; 18-1.7; 24 (small)-1.4; 24 (large)-1.1; 30-.84; 36-.72
Univers 55 (ATF) 6-3.9; 8-3.2; 10-2.7; 12-2.3; 14-2.0; 18-1.7; 24 (small)-1.3; 24 (large)-1.0; 30-.83; 36-.69
Univers 65 (ATF) 6-3.6; 8-3.0; 10-2.5; 12-2.1; 14-1.9; 18-1.6; 24 (small)-1.2; 24 (large)-.97; 30-.77; 36-.64
Univers 75 (ATF) 6-3.4; 8-2.8; 10-2.3;

12-2.0; 14-1.8; 18-1.5; 24 (small)-1.1; 24 (large)-.91; 30-.72; 36-.60
Univers Bold Expanded No. 692 (M) 6-3.08; 8-2.47; 9-2.11; 10-1.83; 14-1.31; 18-1.02; 22-.80; 28-.64; 36-54; 48-.39
Univers Extra Bold No. 696 + It. (M) 6-3.35; 7-2.92; 8-2.71; 8½-2.47; 9-2.32; 10-2.00; 12-1.72; 14-1.46; 16-1.26; 18-1.11; 22-.88; 28-.70; 36-.59; 48-.43
Univers Light Condensed No. 686 + It. 6-5.42; 8-4.38; 9-3.80; 10-3.35; 12-2.85; 14-2.47; 18-1.93; 22-1.54; 28-1.23; 36-1.03; 48-.76
Univers Light No. 685 + It. (M) 6-3.93; 7-3.48; 8-3.16; 8½-2.57; 9-2.71; 10-2.32; 12-2.03; 14-1.72; 16-1.50; 18-1.34; 22-1.06; 28-.85; 36-.71; 48-.52
Univers Medium Expanded No. 688 6-3.08; 8-2.47; 9-2.11; 10-1.83; 14-1.40; 18-.71; 22-.85; 28-.67; 36-.57; 48-.42
Univers Medium Condensed No. 690 + It. (M) 6-4.75; 8-3.93; 9-3.35; 10-3.00; 12-2.59; 14-2.11; 18-1.62; 22-1.26; 28-1.01; 36-.85; 48-.62
Univers Ultra Bold Expanded No. 697 (M) 6-2.78; 8-2.23; 9-1.90; 10-1.65; 14-1.18; 18-.90; 22-.71; 28-.57; 36-.47; 48-.35
Venus Bold (Regular) (B) 8-3.18; 10-2.55; 12-2.15; 14-1.95; 16-1.64; 18-1.49; 24-1.21
Venus Light It. (B) 8-3.56; 10-2.82; 12-2.42; 14-2.06; 16-1.81; 18-1.59; 24-1.36
Venus Medium (Regular) (B) 6-3.6; 8-3.25; 10-2.8; 12-2.35; 14-2.08; 16-1.83; 18-1.62; 24-1.39
Vogue Light & Bold (I) 6-4.; 8-3.56; 10-2.94; 12-2.45; 14-2.14; 18-1.65; 24-1.23
Weiss Roman & It. (I) 8-3.83; 9-3.43; 10-3.19; 11-2.94; 12-2.68; 14-2.25; 16-1.92; 18-1.54
Weiss Roman Bold (B) 8-3.67; 10-3.02; 11-2.78; 12-2.44; 14-2.06; 16-1.8; 18-1.59; 24-2.2
Windsor (B) 10-2.06; 12-1.83; 14-1.42; 18-1.17; 24-1.06
Windsor Light (B) 12-2.02; 14-1.71; 18-1.34; 24-1.05
Windsor Light Cond. (B) 12-2.44; 14-2. 18-1.62; 24-1.29

Character Count Estimator

(Courtesy AD Copyfitter)

STANDARD TYPEWRITER CHARACTER COUNTER

PICA SCALE

5.75-6.01
5.5-5.74
5.25-5.49
5.00-5.24
4.75-4.99
4.5-4.74
4.25-4.49
4.00-4.24
3.90-3.99
3.80-3.89
3.70-3.79
3.60-3.69
3.50-3.59
3.40-3.49
3.30-3.39
3.20-3.29
3.10-3.19
3.00-3.09
2.90-2.99
2.80-2.89

PICA SCALE

2.70-2.79
2.60-2.69
2.50-2.59
2.40-2.49
2.30-2.39
2.20-2.29
2.10-2.19
2.00-2.09
1.90-1.99
1.80-1.89
1.70-1.79
1.60-1.69
1.50-1.59
1.40-1.49
1.30-1.39
1.20-1.29
1.10-1.19
1.00-1.09
.90-.99
.80-.89

Appendix 5

THE ⬤ PROOF/MARKER

This proofreader's guide is adapted from the Quad Proof/Marker, one of the most comprehensive guides available, and is used by permission of Quad Typographers Inc., New York.

deletions

SYMBOL FOR 'TAKE OUT', 'DELETE', 'OMIT' IS ⅋ —A 'DELE'

⅋/	Speak *slow*, if you speak love.	Speak low, if you speak love.
	To know (it) all makes one tolerant. /⅋	*To know all makes one tolerant.*
⅋/	None of his friends /like him.	None of his friends like him.

USE 'HORNS' ⌒ TO INDICATE THAT REMAINDER IS ONE WORD

Come up and see me some*time*. /⅋ ⟶ Come up and see me sometime.

TO DELETE SPACE, SPECIFY BY USING 'LEAD' MARK: #

#⅋/ Con-found all /presents wot eat! ⟶ Con-found all presents wot eat!

See the happy moron, ⟶ *See the happy moron,*

He doesn't give a damn. ⟶ *He doesn't give a damn.*

I wish I were a moron; ⟶ *I wish I were a moron;*

2pt #⅋ — My God! Perhaps I am! ⟶ *My God! Perhaps I am!*

insertions

MARK A CARET ∧ IN TEXT, LETTER OR SYMBOL IN MARGIN

I loaf∧and invite my soul. /e ⟶ I loafe and invite my soul.

not/ *Curfew must∧ring to-night.* ⟶ *Curfew must not ring to-night.*

Never mind her∧go on talking. /⟨;⟩ ⟶ Never mind her; go on talking.

USE 'HORNS' ⌒ TO INDICATE INSERTION JOINS ANOTHER WORD

Meet me by moon∧alone. /⌒light ⟶ Meet me by moonlight alone.

TO INSERT SPACE, INDICATE KIND OR QUANTITY

wd #/ The worm's eye∧point of view. ⟶ The worm's eye point of view.

ADORE:∧to venerate expectantly. /em quad ⟶ ADORE: to venerate expectantly.

Three wise men of Gotham ⟶ *Three wise men of Gotham*

in 2 pt / Went to sea in a bowl. ⟶ *Went to sea in a bowl.*

And if the bowl had been stronger, ⟶ *And if the bowl had been stronger,*

My song would have been longer. ⟶ *My song would have been longer.*

Well roared, Lion! /eq. l/s ⟶ Well roared, Lion!

USE OF SPECIAL PUNCTUATION/MARKS AVOIDS AMBIGUITY

punctuation/marks

SMALL AS A FLYSPECK, A PERIOD MIGHT GET LOST: CIRCLE IT!

⊙/ I never apologize∧ ⟶ I never apologize.

SO TOO WITH AN ELLIPSIS . . . BUT SPACE IT, TOO

∧and thereby hangs a tale. /⊙⊙⊙ ⟶ . . . and thereby hangs a tale.

LOOK-ALIKE COMMA AND APOSTROPHE REQUIRE 'POSITIONING'

This is Dr. Charles' physician.
This is Dr. Charles, physician.

This is Dr. Charles' physician.
This is Dr. Charles, physician.

SO TOO WITH QUOTATION MARKS, SUPERIORS, INFERIORS

"Who saw him die?"
"I," said the Fly.
Area of a circle equals πr.
Chemical formula for water is HO.

"Who saw him die?"
"I," said the Fly.
Area of a circle equals πr^2.
Chemical formula for water is H_2O.

CIRCLING THE COLONS CAN HELP TOO

Love thyself last cherish
　　　those hearts that hate thee

Love thyself last: cherish
　　　those hearts that hate thee;

NOTE THE DISTINCTION BETWEEN HYPHENS AND DASHES

In two words: impossible!
What shall we do or go fishing?

In two words: im-possible!
What shall we do—or go fishing?

RARER, BUT DIFFERENT, IS THE 'EN' DASH (NOTE ALL 3 BELOW)

World-War I—1914 1918

World-War I—1914–1918

TO LESSEN CONFUSION, LABEL EQUALS SIGN AND MINUS SIGN

$3x^2$　$5x - 11$　0

$3x^2 - 5x - 11 = 0$

OFTEN '?' AND '!' ARE TAKEN AS 'ASIDES'; SO MARK THEM 'SET'

Hath not thy rose a thorn
Like—but oh how different

Hath not thy rose a thorn?
Like—but oh how different!

changes

STRIKE OUT UNWANTED CHARACTER; SHOW NEW ONE IN MARGIN

O! thereby hangs a tail.
Kissing don't last; cookery do!
There is a spirit if the woods.
All the world's a stage.
We are but amused.
The superfluous is very necessary.
Nature is usually Wrong.

O! thereby hangs a tail.
Kissing don't last; cookery do!
There is a spirit in the woods.
All the world's a stage.
We are not amused.
The superfluous is very necessary.
Nature is usually wrong.

transpositions

SIMPLE TRANSPOSITIONS REQUIRE SIMPLE MARKING

'Tis as cheap sitting as standing.
There's two to words that bargain.
This is the end of the beginning.
Love him, or leave him alone!
Going towards my boat, I was ex-
ceedingly surprised with the very
plain print of a man's naked foot
on the shore, which was to be seen.

'Tis as cheap sitting as standing.
There's two words to that bargain.
This is the beginning of the end.
Love him, or leave him alone!
Going towards my boat, I was ex-
ceedingly surprised with the print
of a man's naked foot on the shore,
which was very plain to be seen.

COMPLICATED TRANSPOSITIONS REQUIRE REWRITING

typographic style

ALTERATION TO ROMAN IS STRAIGHTFORWARD

Fortune aids the brave.

Fortune aids the brave.

TO RESET IN ITALIC, UNDERSCORE ONCE

Twinkle, twinkle, little star.

Twinkle, *twinkle*, little star.

TO MAKE IT SMALL CAPS, UNDERSCORE TWICE

Th'artillery of words. /sc

Th'ARTILLERY of words.

FOR CAPITALS, USE THREE UNDERSCORES

the unimaginable touch of type. /caps

all caps/ once upon a time.

The Unimaginable Touch of Type.
ONCE UPON A TIME.

NOTE THE TECHNIQUE FOR CAPS AND SMALL CAPS

a room of one's own. /c+sc

A ROOM OF ONE'S OWN.

STRIKE ONLY THE·FIRST INTENDED LOWER-CASE LETTER . . .

ulc/ THE SILVER APPLES OF THE MOON
THE GOLDEN APPLES OF THE SUN /ulc

The silver apples of the moon.
The Golden Apples of the Sun.

. . . NOT THE WHOLE LOT!

LIARS NEED GOOD MEMORIES.

(illegible)

FOR BOLDFACE, USE A WAVY-LINE UNDERSCORE

BF/ Et tu, Brute!

Et tu, Brute!

AND FOR ITALIC BOLDFACE, COMBINE THE STRAIGHT AND WAVY

'Nay, we are seven!' /ital BF

'Nay, we are seven!'

TO SPELL OUT ABBREVIATIONS OR FIGURES

Life in these U.S. /sp

sp/ Bread & butter.

A fool at 40 is a fool indeed. /sp

Life in these United States.
Bread and butter.
A fool at forty is a fool indeed.

TO INDICATE DESIRED USE OF LIGATURES ('TIED' LETTERS)

Off . . file . . flag . . office . . waffle /ligs

Off . . file . . flag . . office . . waffle

FOR KERNED, NOTCHED LETTERS (OR LOGOTYPES)

kern Twice is once too often.

Twice is once too often.

WHEN A LETTER, WORD, OR LINE IS MIS-MATCHED (A 'WRONG FONT')

Oh Captain! my Captain! /wf

wf/ Man is the measure of all things.

He who has never hoped
can never despair. — wf

Oh Captain! my Captain!
Man is the measure of all things.
He who has never hoped
can never despair.

spacing and leading

LEAD # IS THE SPACE ADDED BETWEEN LINES

Ask yourself whether you are happy, and you cease to be so. in 6pt #

Ask yourself whether you are happy, and you cease to be so.

A SETTING WITH NO LEAD IS CALLED 'SOLID'

solid (Sword of Common Sense!
Our surest gift.

Sword of Common Sense!
Our surest gift.

CLOSE UP WORD SPACE—ENTIRELY

Weak as is a break ing wave. /⌒

Weak as is a breaking wave.

CLOSE WORD SPACE; BUT LEAVE SOME

Accept a miracle, instead of wit.

Accept a miracle, instead of wit.

INSERT, OR INCREASE, SPACE

It is love that I am seeking for. /wd #

add #/ Despise not any man.

It is love that I am seeking for.
Despise not any man.

REDUCE WORD SPACE

Man is a tool-making animal. /less #

Man is a tool-making animal.

EQUALIZE WORD SPACE

eq # / The more laws, the less justice.

The more laws, the less justice.

LETTERSPACE

I cannot bear men and women. /l/s

I cannot bear men and women.

INDENT AS MANY EM QUADS AS SHOWN

□□□ ⊐ All professions are
conspiracies against the laity.

　　　All professions are
conspiracies against the laity.

paragraphing and position

NO NEW PARAGRAPH (ALSO 'RUN IN' OR 'RUN ON')

run in

This is not the end.
It is not even the beginning of
the end.
But it is, perhaps, the end of
the beginning.

　　　This is not the end. It is not
even the beginning of the end. But
it is, perhaps, the end of the
beginning.

BEGIN NEW PARAGRAPH

¶□/

The cook was a good cook, as
cooks go. And as cooks go, she
went.

　　　The cook was a good cook, as
cooks go.
　　　And as cooks go, she went.

INDENT PARAGRAPH (STATE HOW MUCH)

¶□□

Remember that the most beautiful
things in the world are the most
useless; peacocks and lilies, for
instance.

　　　Remember that the most beautiful things in the world are the
most useless; peacocks and lilies,
for instance.

FLUSH PARAGRAPH

flush ¶

[I intend no modification of
my oft-expressed personal wish
that all men everywhere could be free.

I intend no modification of my oft-
expressed personal wish that all
men everywhere could be free.

HANGING INDENTION

hang indent 1 em

If there be any man cursed with
the itch to compress a whole book
into a page, a whole page into a
phrase, and that phrase into a
word, it is I.

If there be any man cursed with
　the itch to compress a whole
　book into a page, a whole page
　into a phrase, and that phrase
　into a word, it is I.

RUN OVER (START NEW LINE)

run over

He who can, does. He who cannot,
teaches.

He who can, does.
He who cannot, teaches.

RUN BACK (PICK UP)

A fool and his words
are soon parted;
a man of genius—
and his money.

pick up

A fool and his words are soon
parted; a man of genius—and
his money.

RESET TO NEW MEASURE (STATE IT)

reset ×12 picas

The humblest citizen of all the land, when clad in the armor of a righteous cause, is stronger than all the hosts of error.

The humblest citizen of all the land, when clad in the armor of a righteous cause, is stronger than all the hosts of error.

MOVE...LEFT...RIGHT...UP...DOWN...(BRACKET SHOWS DIRECTION)

flush [Uncover, dogs, and lap.
Every bullet has its billet.] *flush*
align An undevout astronomer is mad.
Who can refute a sneer? *align*

Uncover, dogs, and lap.
Every bullet has its billet.
An undevout astronomer is mad.
Who can refute a sneer?

ALIGN OR FLUSH...VERTICALLY...HORIZONTALLY

flush left ‖ Woodman, spare that tree!
Touch not a single bough!
In youth it sheltered me,
And I'll protect it now. ‖ *flush right*
align Are we downhearted? No!

Woodman, spare that tree!
Touch not a single bough!
In youth it sheltered me,
And I'll protect it now.
Are we downhearted? No!

CENTER...INDIVIDUALLY...OR AS A UNIT

] Sudden as sweet [*center over 2nd line*
Come the expected feet.
He snatched the thunderbolt
from heaven,
soon the sceptres
from tyrants.) *center on 15 picas*
] Alas! my everlasting peace
Is broken into pieces. [*center as a unit on (15)*

Sudden as sweet
Come the expected feet.
He snatched the thunderbolt
from heaven,
soon the sceptres
from tyrants.
Alas! my everlasting peace
Is broken into pieces.

miscellany

'STET' MEANS 'LET IT STAND'...I'VE CHANGED MY MIND!

We're here because we're here. *stet*
stet room Come away, O human child! /h *stet*
Keep yourself to yourself.
Neither a borrower nor a lender be.) *stet line*

We're here because we're here.
Come away, O human child!
Keep yourself *to* yourself.
Neither a borrower nor a lender be.

THERE IS AN 'OUT'. SEE COPY, AND SET ACCORDINGLY

osc/ Cry, baby, cry. Put your finger
tell your mother it wasn't I.

Cry, baby, cry. Put your finger
in your eye and tell your mother
it wasn't I.

MARK MULTIPLE CORRECTIONS IN THE SAME ORDER AS THE DESIRED
CHANGES, SEPARATING THEM BY SLASHES; AND USING BOTH MARGINS

God to theant, thou slugard; /d/#/g
tr#/o considerfer ways, and be wise.
A harmless necessary catch. €/? //d/o

Go to the ant, thou sluggard;
consider her ways, and be wise.
A harmless (necessary) cat.

TO QUESTION (OR QUERY) SOMETHING...

Qu— You're not a man, your a machine. *you're?*

BUT...HAVE THE QUERY ANSWERED BEFORE RETURNING PROOF!

Appendix 6

Alternative Faces

The following list is a selection of type faces and their "look-alike" faces which are similar in design. This list was compiled from the catalogs of Alphatype, ATF, Compugraphic, Graphic Systems, Intertype, ITC, Ludlow, Mecanorma, Mergenthaler, Monotype, Photon, Type Films of Chicago and Zipatone. Two sources were particularly valuable: the Spec-Liner published by the Western Typesetting Company and the Encyclopedia of Typefaces.

Alphy, Ad Contour, Archie

Alternate Gothic, Trade Gothic, News Gothic

Antique, Egyptian, Clarendon, Consort, Rockwell, Stymie

Aries, Dorsch Black, Fat Albert, Leo Solid

Arthur, King Arthur, Artline, Guinevere

Astoria, Comstock

Avant Garde, Avante, Vanguard

Baskerville, Beaumont, Baskerline

Blippo, Harry, Poppo, Bubble

Bodoni, Didoni, Vixen, Pistilli Roman, Brunswick

Bowlegged, Chicken Noodle, Drip

Busorama, Omnibus, Buster

Cairo, Memphis, Karnak

Caledonia, Caledo, California, Laurel, Edinburgh, Highland, Cornelia

Cartoon, Studio, Fresko

Celebration, Wycombe

Celtic, Forum Flair

Charleston, Lautrec Light

Cheltenham, Winchester, Gloucester, Cheltonian

Cinema, Hollywood

Cloister Old Style, Jenson

Computer, Moore Computer, Data Process, Digital

Comstock, Astoria

Contempo, Deutsch Black, Deep Black

Cooper Black, Ludlow Black, Goudy Extra Bold

Coronet, Trafton, Park Avenue, Belair

Corvinus, Skyline, Eden, Coronation, Glamour, Quirinus

Dominante, Dominance, Dominion, Darling

Dorsch Black, Aries, Leo Solid, Fat Albert, Taurus

Eros, Smoke, Watusi

Eurostile, Eurogothic, Microgramma, Gramma, Commerce Gothic, Bank Gothic, Stationer's Gothic

Fat Albert, Aries, Dorsch, Leo, Taurus

Fat Chance, Sonomiro, Marianna Black

Firenze, Florence

Flatback, Baby Arbuckle, Buxom, Lean Back

Folio, Helvetica, Caravelle, Video Spectra

Fritz Quadrata, Diamond

Futura, Spartan, Europe, Fotura, Utica

Garamond, Grenada, Garaldus, Garamont, Jannon, Granjon

Ginger, Eden, Eagle, Echo, Envoy, Vanity

Goudy Extra Bold, Ludlow Black, Rugged Black, Cooper Black

Grizzly, Bear, Kabel Extra Bold

Grouch, Growl, Grumpy

Guinevere, King Arthur, Arthur, Artline

Happy Sid, Jolly Roger, Jolly Martin

Harry, Blippo, Bubble, Joel, Poppo, Rocky

Helvetica, Vega, Boston, Claro, Corvus, Galaxy, Geneva, Helios, American Gothic, Ag Book, Newton, Megaron

Herbie, Oboe

Jenson, Italian Old Style, Golden Type, Zilver Type

Karnak, Memphis, Cairo

Jolly Roger, Happy Sid

Kabel, Cabel, Kabello

Lautrec, Charleston, Roberta

Marianna Black, Fat Chance, Sonomiro

Melior, Medallion, Piccadilly, Ruxton, Melnor, Dominance, Uranus, Ballardville, Hanover, Lyra, Mallard, Ventura

Memphis, Cairo, Girder, Karnak, Stymie

Microgramma, Eurostile

News Gothic, Trade Gothic, Toledo

Nouveau, Toulouse

Optima, Chelmsford, Oracle, Orleans, Musica, Ursa, Zenith

Palatino, Palateno, Elegante, Patina, Andover, Palladium, Pontiac, Michelangelo, Sistina

Park Avenue, Belair, Coronet, Trafton

Playbill, French Antique, Figaro, Pro Arte

Post Old Roman, Pabst Old Style, Kolonia, Columbia, Buffalo, Morland, Blanchard, Roycroft

Record Gothic, Trade Gothic

Shaggy Text, Berlin Flair, Pen Flair

Smoke, Eros, Watusi

Spartan, Photura, Sirius, Techno, Tempo, Twentieth Century, Utica, Futura

Spring, Radiant Flair, Rockwell, Cairo, Memphis Alexandria

Stymie, Memphis

Toulouse, Nouveau

Trade Gothic, Alternate Gothic, News Gothic, Toledo

Univers, Versatile, Boston, Galaxy

Index

Entries in italics indicate typefaces